ADVANCE

Love You, ̣ ̣ ̣

In *Love Your Neighbor*, Deacon Eddie Ensley has once again offered practical guidance on effectively living out the Christian life in faith, hope, and love, by living and living up to the second great commandment—love of neighbor. His multiplicity of memorable illustrative stories and rich pastoral and prayerful experiences demonstrate that the follow-up question the lawyer should have asked Jesus in Luke 10:29 was not the minimizing and self-justifying "And who is my neighbor?" but the eminently practical and prayerfully self-transforming: "And how is my neighbor? How do I love my neighbor?"

—Monsignor Christopher Schreck, rector/president,
Pontifical College Josephinum

I have known Eddie Ensley since he was a very young man, and he has always had passion and skill for healing real people with their real sufferings...you are being taught by a master who has practiced this healing work for most of his life, along with his faithful coworker, Deacon Robert Herman.

—Richard Rohr, O.F.M., author, *Eager to Love*

John Donne wrote, "No man is an island." In *Love Your Neighbor*, Deacon Eddie Ensley reminds us how essential loving relationships are for our health and happiness, while offering powerful insights into how these same relationships flow from and lead back to the love God has for us.

—Silas Henderson, managing editor of Abbey Press
and *Deacon Digest* magazine

Love Your Neighbor is a how-to book that is not only practical but, as only Ensley can do, touches the reader on a deeply emotional level. Ensley deftly blends spirituality, psychology, Christian history, and story to illustrate his message. He reminds us that through imaginative prayer and silence, we can access God's healing power to help us grow in love for everyone, including ourselves. I highly recommend this book to anyone who is serious about the spiritual journey and wants practical help in improving his or her relationships.

—Judy Esway, MA, CT, author, *Real Life, Real Spirituality*

I am honored to provide my recommendation for this book *Love Your Neighbor*. Dr. Eddie Ensley is one of the mightiest men of God that I have ever met. It stands to reason, then, that I am thrilled with this book. It addresses the two deepest needs. First, it helps those who are struggling with a difficult relationship/situation. It lights the path to *healing and reconciliation*. Second, it provides wisdom to Christians (counselors, pastors, leaders, etc.) who are trying to help others resolve relationship problems. You will be helped and blessed by this book—blessed beyond measure!

—Bishop Richard G. Arno, Ph.D., founder,
National Christian Counselors Association

I have known Deacon Eddie since my first days as a Catholic through the ministry of SCRC, the Catholic Charismatic ministry community in Southern California. His insights into the integration of the contemplative, relational, and charismatic spiritualties have always been groundbreaking. Now as a Catholic deacon, Eddie brings a further pastoral insight as well. Focusing on love through storied experience as well as study, Eddie fleshes out the theory of God's love through human pastoral experience. It is a good read.

—John Michael Talbot, founder, Brothers and Sisters of Charity

LOVE YOUR NEIGHBOR

Love Your Neighbor

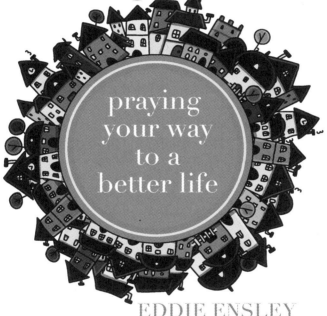

praying
your way
to a
better life

EDDIE ENSLEY

Franciscan
MEDIA
Cincinnati, Ohio

Stories included here that involve people other than the author make use of composites created from his experience in his ministry. Any similarity to individuals known to readers is coincidental.

Unless otherwise noted, Scripture passages have been taken from *New Revised Standard Version Bible,* copyright ©1989 by the Division of Christian Education of the National Council of the Churches of Christ in the U.S.A., and used by permission. All rights reserved.

Cover and book design by Mark Sullivan
Cover illustration © Kudryashka I iStock

LIBRARY OF CONGRESS CATALOGING-IN-PUBLICATION DATA
Ensley, Eddie.
Love your neighbor : praying your way to a better life / Eddie Ensley.
pages cm
Includes bibliographical references.
ISBN 978-1-61636-939-2 (alk. paper)
1. Love—Religious aspects—Christianity. 2. Interpersonal relations—Religious aspects—Christianity. 3. Friendship—Religious aspects—Christianity. 4. Intercessory prayer. I. Title.
BV4639.E56 2015
241'.4—dc23
                                    2015027535

ISBN 978-1-61636-939-2

Published by Franciscan Media
28 W. Liberty St.
Cincinnati, OH 45202
www.FranciscanMedia.org

Printed in the United States of America.
Printed on acid-free paper.
15 16 17 18 19 5 4 3 2 1

For Bill Beatty and the Alleluia Community,
who touched and shaped my life.

And in memory of Monsignor Josiah Chatham
and for his congregation at St. Richard's parish in Jackson
who provided me my first taste of a Catholic parish.

~CONTENTS~

~introduction~

Do you believe prayer can transform relationships?

For a full week I had dreaded giving a retreat to the faculty of a Midwestern Catholic girls' school. I kept hoping they would cancel, but they didn't. Five minutes into my first talk of the morning, I knew my fears were justified. Grim, stony faces glared at me. The audience reminded me of a pot of water on the edge of boiling over.

A week earlier the pastor had called to tell me that the faculty was in meltdown. The new principal had been pushing hard for the teachers to improve their teaching skills and lesson plans. A number of the faculty reacted with resentment. At one faculty meeting, the tension erupted in a shouting match between faculty loyal to the new principal and those opposing her. Afterward, unfounded rumors flew that the board would fire several of the teachers or replace the principal.

During the lunch break, a handful of teachers on both sides of the dispute shared their stories with me. I had planned to give a talk on prayer that afternoon. Suddenly, it came to me: instead of *talking* about prayer, we needed *to pray*. That afternoon we needed words and thoughts from God to penetrate our hearts.

I first gave a brief introduction to *Lectio Divina,* an age-old way of prayerfully reading the Scriptures. While *Lectio Divina* is primarily used for individual prayer, it can also be adapted for use by groups. I played a CD of a slow version of Pachelbel's "Canon in D" in the background. After a few minutes of listening to the music, we took about ten minutes to pray some Our Fathers to calm our souls. Then I started reading slowly from 1 Corinthians 13, pausing when I felt the gentle touch of the Spirit move over the group. I could tell by their faces that those in the group were settling into a deep state of prayer.

I read the Scripture passage once more, slowly and with pauses, giving time for the words to sink in. This time I repeated words and phrases that seemed "anointed" by a special touch of the Spirit. "Love is patient," I repeated slowly, then paused in a long silence. "Love is kind. It is not irritable or resentful." I paused again. Next I read from John 13, the passage that describes Jesus washing the feet of the disciples. In the second reading of the passage, I slowly repeated the phrase "wash one another's feet."

When I had finished the reading, we spent ten minutes in silent prayer. After a few moments, one of the middle-aged teachers spontaneously broke the quiet. Tears coursing down her face, her voice choked as she addressed the group. "I regret so much my outburst at the last faculty meeting." She turned to the principal. "You didn't deserve the cruel words I aimed at you. You are a decent human being who loves the students as much as I do."

The principal walked over and embraced the teacher, tears streaming from her eyes as well. The principal addressed the group. "Please forgive me. I could certainly be far more sensitive to your feelings and opinions as I implement these new policies."

One teacher after the other expressed regret and the strong wish for the faculty to be reconciled. The presence of God filled the air; there was hardly a dry eye in the room.

This is just one of numerous times I have seen prayer and spirituality bring healing to hurting relationships. Prayer can help bring separated hearts back together again and, in the process, deepen the original relationships.

I recently read the story of a California father, David Patterson, who had abandoned his daughter, now thirteen, before she was born. When he heard this daughter's only kidney was failing, the Spirit stirred within him and he wrote a letter offering one of his own. He penned his letter from a prison cell where he was serving a seven-year sentence for burglary. He told her, "If you can forgive me, I will do my best to be the daddy I should have been a long time ago." The transplant surgery took place at the University of California at San Francisco Medical Center.[1]

Such a gesture to restore a relationship can be called as much a miracle as the healing of the man born blind in the Gospel. Only God can lead us to such gestures that catapult the healing of a relationship to whole new level.

My own family experienced such a miracle. My maternal grandfather, Walter Crittenden, abandoned his four children to an orphanage when my mother was just nine. He never wrote my mother the entire time she was in the orphan's home. This abandonment was especially vicious, since, in his own way, my grandfather was a man of great tenderness, and my mother's early experiences of him were precious. Her anger at him grew immense. When she was married and an adult she would reluctantly let him visit, but she made it clear he was not truly welcome.

Before her father's death, when I was well into my adulthood, bitterness would well up in my mother. I remember one time she said, "I am not all that sure I want to go to heaven, because my father would be there and I don't want to spend eternity with him."

However, when Granddaddy Walt was dying of lung cancer in his early eighties, Mother listened to the soft voice of God in her heart and tended him gently, babying him with great affection as he had once babied her when she was little. Mother's reaching out to him in the last days of his life was nothing less than a miracle. It drained the bitterness away and let them be father and daughter again. It took prayer on my mother's part to come to that point; she let God move her beyond her comfort zone.

God can lead all of us to make wondrous gestures of love. Through prayer, we can talk with him about our relationships and let him guide us.

Life is not a solo journey. Even before we were born, we were in relationship to others—first our birth mother, then others who came into our lives. Some relationships are casual: the bank teller, the mail carrier, the store clerk. Some relationships are much more substantial; they touch our souls. Among them are close friends, relatives, spouses, teachers, mentors, and coworkers. It is these deeper relationships we will focus on in this book. One way to look at relationships is to see each life as an individual thread. By itself one thread is not impressive, but when we weave the threads of many lives together, a beautiful textured cloth can emerge, giving all our lives meaning and purpose.

Whenever we make time to build positive relationships, not only are our relationships enriched, but our vitality and health are improved. We move beyond merely existing to truly living. Relationships allow God to sculpt us into the fully alive human beings God intended us to be from all eternity.

Yet, relationships are often challenging. Young people learn math, reading, and writing in school. Driving classes prepare adolescents for the road by teaching the basics of operating an automobile. Society trains us step-by-step for many of the important things of life. Yet, there are no prerequisites for dating and friendship. Relationship skills are mostly absent from our education.

People hunger for help in their relationships. I googled "relationship advice" and got over twenty million results. Some people move from one troubled relationship to the next. They try to fill emotional needs from unresolved earlier relationships and past wounds. As a result, they keep finding the same kind of person and encounter abuse or other emotional issues over and over again. Most of what we know about relationship skills comes from those who raised us: our parents and our caretakers. Yet with more than fifty percent of marriages ending in divorce and so many dysfunctional families, these models often fall far short of adequate.[2]

The media has a major influence on how we learn relationship skills. Romantic movies often present just the infatuation and honeymoon stage of marriage, rarely following relationships through the years. In addition, tabloid-style news frequently report on celebrity relationships. While there are exceptions, too many celebrities engage in throw-away relationships without real commitment, providing a poor example for the young people who view them as role models.

Cultivating God-filled relationships is important in all facets of life. This is why I wrote this book. Each chapter will feature reflections on some aspect of human relationships, beginning with our personal relationship with God, our formative experience as children, developing spiritual friendships, cultivating professional relationships, and keeping God at the center of married and family life. The second portion of the book will focus on particular challenges commonly faced in relationships. These include difficulties in communication, dealing with conflict and the need for forgiveness and affirmation.

Each chapter will also include a "Time for Healing Prayer" section: a prayer, a Scripture passage to ponder, and a guided meditation that uses memory and imagination. Journaling questions round out the chapter.

Drawing from the Scriptures and our rich Christian heritage, this book will gently draw you into meditations that invite God to heal, restore, and deepen your relationships.

~chapter one~

LOVING
God

Something was missing in my life. I was studying to be a Presbyterian minister at Belhaven College in Jackson, Mississippi. Day after day I pored over dense philosophical books and scholarly Scripture-study tomes. I read far more than was required, searching hard for something to touch my soul. I read daily about the love of God from masterful theologians like Karl Barth and Dietrich Bonhoeffer. My head was crammed full of knowledge, but, at least for the time being, my heart felt empty. To be sure, I had felt God's love before, both as a child and as a young man, but now I journeyed through a wasteland. My inner landscape was as dry as the desert. I yearned for something more.

Then something happened that was to change my life forever. I passed through Selma, Alabama, after spending spring break with my parents in Columbus, Georgia. One of my high school teachers, who had remained a friend and mentor, had been a part of the Catholic Church in Selma growing up. She said I should visit the beautiful church there someday. As I passed through Selma, I decided I would stop and do just that. Sheer curiosity about what it was like in one of those Catholic Churches was part of my motivation. For the first time in my life, I set foot in an empty Catholic Church. To my surprise; it looked very much like a Presbyterian Church.

The difference, however, is what mattered. Up front was a gold box. I didn't know what it was, but I felt drawn toward it. It was as though God whispered in my ear saying, "Come closer."

I sat down in a pew directly in front of that box. At that moment love flooded my heart; tenderness, melting compassion, and comfort rose up within me. Warmth coursed through my body. A quiet came over me that was nothing less than the peace of God. Time ceased to exist.

This love was no theological abstraction. Rather it was a great stream pouring through me from God's inmost being; a love that knows no pause. A memory was born that I would relish and draw on the rest of my life.

That moment sent me on a five-year journey that would end with my becoming Catholic. Even though I did not know what a tabernacle was, much less the Blessed Sacrament, Christ reached out of the tabernacle and kissed my heart with his love. After that experience I grew more tenderhearted. It was easier to love others and be sensitive to their needs and feelings. I now knew I had a great reservoir of compassion, God's loving-kindness, to help me empathize with those around me. What started as a personal experience of God became one that included relationships with others.

We experience God in more ways than through a tabernacle. We can experience him in Scripture, in churches of other faith expressions, in creation, and in our relationships. This love of God is the source for our love of others. Being a Christian means being in relationships. Jesus said that the two greatest commandments are to love God with all our heart, soul, mind, and strength and to love our neighbors as ourselves (see Matthew 22:37–40; Mark 12:29–31). As many have said, Christianity boils down to a loving, personal, "vertical" relationship with God through his Son, Jesus Christ, and loving "horizontal" relationships with fellow humans.

The feeling of God's love is not always as intense as my experience in that empty church in Selma that spring day. We all pass through times when our feelings turn dry for a season; that's normal in an ongoing relationship with God. But we know through faith God is boundless love, an eternity of caring. "God is love, and those who abide in love abide in God" (1 John 4:16). However, the statement "God is love" by itself is not enough.

For the statement "God is love" to catch our attention and change us, it must be fleshed out, become approachable and incarnate. This is exactly what happened in Jesus. In him the endless ocean of love that is God became touchable, approachable, and real. Infinite, ineffable love became an everyday love, a love we could relate to.

From his earliest days, Jesus experienced a mysterious love all around him and in the center of his being. At some point, in the most natural way, he began to call this love *Abba*, the Aramaic word for "Daddy." This was the image that most fully expressed his relationship to that love. Later, he came to know that the love he called "Daddy" was also his own innermost identity. Through the earthly relationship he had with others, and through the story that was his life, he made that love real for us.

He can relate to us humans because he was fully human, coming forth from our human race. Like us, he lived the life of a human being. He knew joy as we know joy. He ate, drank, and slept as we do. He grew hungry, tired, and stressed. He felt the ordinary needs of the human heart. He was hurt by malice. He yearned for love. He prayed, laughed, and wept. His heart widened in the presence of friends, and was torn when friends deserted him. He knows our burdens, suffers in our losses, and knows what we need. In short, he knows how to relate to us.

God shows us his love in the way Jesus related to those around him. Jesus turned the world's understanding of things upside down. He demonstrated that his Father loved with a scandalous love—prostitutes, drunkards, tax collectors were special objects of his passionate caring. He was the shepherd who would leave the ninety-nine sheep for the one lost sheep; the father who embraced and kissed the returning son who had squandered all that the father had given him. He was the woman who swept the house clean searching for the lost coin. Jesus himself showed that searching love of God by mingling with sinners, and even having people hurl at him the accusation of being a glutton and drunkard. By the way Jesus lived his life; he showed what God was like, reaching out to people in the deepest level of their woundedness, loving us in the midst of our humanity.

Augustine wrote, "The love with which we love God and love one another is the same love."[3] Mature spirituality involves experiencing God in human relationships as well as in solitude. Prayer that moves us away from people can become escapism. Prayer and people belong together. Relationship is not a means to a goal; it is the goal.

Diana Hagee tells this story about the trenches in World War I France:

> Two friends in the American army were caught in the muddy hell of trench warfare. They were commanded to charge over the barbed wire; the resistance was ferocious, and they retreated. One of the two friends was seriously wounded and left behind. The other friend, disobeying a direct order from his officer, went after his wounded companion. When he returned to the trench with his friend on his shoulder, his friend was dead and he himself had been mortally wounded while dragging him back. The officer said, "It wasn't worth it, was it?" The soldier looked him in the eye and said, "Yes, it was worth it, because when I got there he said, 'Jim, I knew you would come.'"[4]

We relate to one another not to win a war, not to implement a program, or finish a project, but because it's our eternal calling. In the midst of the earthly coarseness of daily life, in the midst of their humanity, people can become channels of God's love.

Think about the people who have revealed God's love for you. Perhaps they don't consciously know this. Perhaps they are not even outwardly religious people, but they have been a sign of his love and a means of his love. They incarnate, enflesh, and make God's caring tangible. Many little saviors have incarnated the love of the one Savior. The apostle Paul, in beginning and closing his letters, often said, "I think of you whenever I pray to God" (see Philippians 1:3). He could also say, "You are to me the aroma of Christ" (see 2 Corinthians 2:15). This concrete love, made flesh in Jesus, is the basis of all our other love.

We encounter God in prayer and we can encounter people in prayer. When we pray we should not run from the people who make up the fabric of daily living, but take them into our prayer. They are fuel for meditation. They are grist for the mill. Prayer thrives on the horizontal dimension. Like Paul, we can remember people in our prayer, the times of closeness and strength. Remembering brings those healing times into the present. In our prayer we can experience again the people who have been to us channels of God's love. We can practice loving people in our prayer. We can bring hurt relationships to a loving God for mending.

When we pray we take a sunbath in God's love and allow that love to transfigure the fabric of our being. A special way of soaking up God's kindness is through imaginative meditation. Imaginative prayer is found in the Hebrew Scriptures and throughout the Christian tradition.

In Psalm 23, the psalmist places himself in green pastures, walks by still waters, and walks through the dark valley where the Lord is with him. The Church fathers and mothers used guided imaginative meditations. In the Middle Ages friars led congregations in them for emotional healing. It was said that the healing was so profound that tears traced down every face.

Each of us, no matter how difficult our lives, has memories of God blessing us or God touching us. Such memories can include your first Communion, having a child, your marriage or ordination, or times you looked out at nature and the scene was so beautiful you said to yourself, "This is so beautiful, there must be a God."

These memories form a great treasure chest full of beauty. We need to take those memories out of the box and experience God's power to touch us once again with power. Luke's Gospel tells us, "Mary remembered all these things and pondered them in her heart." We too need to ponder in our hearts the mighty acts of God in our lives and in our world. We can ponder the way relationships, at times in the past, have been a channel of God's love. We can draw from the strength of those memories. Then we will surely encounter God's power to heal and deepen our relationships in the here and now.

Jeff and Rachel combined memory and imagination in their prayer and it helped save and restore their marriage. This couple had made it. They lived in a huge, five-bedroom house in the best part of town. Jeff was a contractor who loved his work. He not only made profits on his projects; he made them works of art. Buoyant, always confident, he seemed consumed by his work. He exuded constant excitement, at least on the surface.

His wife was a different story. Rachel seemed quiet; the dark rings under her eyes glared out at you. Her face was clouded with uneasiness. On one of the few days that Jeff was home early enough to eat supper with her, she sat him down and shocked him with the news that she would be seeking a divorce. She told him that she no longer had a role in his life, that he treated her as secondary, and that she felt ignored. Her complaints were typical of those who are not affirmed and treated as full persons. At one time she had a career as a guidance counselor in a school, but they made it in such a big way financially that she stayed home to be with the children. Now the children were grown and Jeff had little time for her concerns; no time for their life together.

As Jeff listened, he clutched the arms of his chair, his stomach clenched tight with an icy fear. Alone a day later, out of desperation, he began to pray. He recalled some of the ways of prayer and meditation that he had been learning from his church. He put on music and lay down on his bed, letting the gentle melody absorb some of the hurt he felt. As a stillness came over him, he took time to remember; he recalled the struggles he and Rachel faced when they were young, the giddy joys, the financial hurdles they had overcome together, their closeness.

For several days in a row he took time for prayerful remembering, and gradually a change came over him. His prayer melted away much of his defensiveness, his armor, the need to be right. He did something unusual for him. He admitted that most of Rachel's complaints were true. He had failed her. His eyes brimming with tears, he asked Rachel to forgive him. Out of his heart he said, "I want it to be like those early times again. And I know I have ignored you."

All of this stunned Rachel. She couldn't remember when she had seen him so defenseless, so vulnerable—it warmed a bit the coldness in her heart toward him. The strength of the memories that he shared evoked the warm feelings of their early marriage. By telling her what he experienced in meditation, he called her into the experience. She also began to weep, and a stillness came over them, a quiet full of comfort. Somehow they knew they would make it.

They would have a lot of work to do for their marriage to thrive again; the path ahead would be hard. But they also knew that they possessed the strength of many beautiful memories. And they knew that they had God's love. The God who was so much a part of their beginnings was there with them now. That day was the beginning of healing for them.

TIME FOR HEALING PRAYER
A Prayer

Dear Lord, you came so close to us in Jesus. In him you showed how to relate to God and others. As we strive to love others, show us we are not alone. Your hand in ours, you accompany us on our journey of loving and relating to others if we but ask you to join us. You pour your unfathomable love upon us, help us to be conduits of this love to others. You are the sunlight that heals as it warms. Help us be mirrors that reflect this light to others.

SCRIPTURE TO PONDER

Read the following Scripture slowly so that it sinks in. Let the words find a hiding place in your heart. If part of the passage really touches or speaks to you, slowly read that passage over again, savoring it. Let the Scripture lead you into the stillness of God.

> If then there is any encouragement in Christ, any conso-
> lation from love, any sharing in the Spirit, any compas-
> sion and sympathy, make my joy complete: be of the same
> mind, having the same love, being in full accord and of
> one mind. Do nothing from selfish ambition or conceit,
> but in humility regard others as better than yourselves.
> Let each of you look not to your own interests, but to the
> interests of others. Let the same mind be in you that was
> in Christ Jesus,
> who, though he was in the form of God,
>   did not regard equality with God
> as something to be exploited,
> but emptied himself,

taking the form of a slave,
being born in human likeness.
And being found in human form,
he humbled himself
and became obedient to the point of death—
even death on a cross.

Therefore God also highly exalted him
and gave him the name
that is above every name,
so that at the name of Jesus
every knee should bend,
in heaven and on earth and under the earth,
and every tongue should confess
that Jesus Christ is Lord,
to the glory of God the Father. (Philippians 2:1–11)

GUIDED MEDITATION

In your imagination, picture Jesus standing beside you. You take his hand. You feel the place where the nail was and you are reminded that that is how much he loves you. Healing warmth from his hand passes up from your hand into your arm, into your entire body until you are totally flooded by warm healing love, soul and body.

If some unease has developed in you, there is no need to dig for it. Instead, tell Jesus about that unease and let him comfort and heal you.

Carry your thoughts back to times when other people have counted you better than themselves, have looked to your interests, have really emptied themselves in a selfless way in order to understand you, to know your needs. Remember the sights, the sounds, and the feelings. How did you feel? Did this help you blossom? How did they go about it? Take some time to remember.

Now recall some times when you have acted selflessly, reaching out of yourself to understand others, times when you counted other people's interests equal to your own. What did that feel like? How did they respond to you?

Ponder some people who make up your life right now. Are you going outside yourself to know and understand what's important to them? In Paul's words, are you "counting them better than yourself"?

Now, form an image of emptying out yourself in order to know and respond to these people's needs. Of course, realize that what we imagine in prayer may take time to manifest itself in our lives. Be gentle with yourself; be forgiving of yourself. It will take a while for this prayer and this imagery to help you love like that. Know that every step of the way you have the helping grace, the comfort, the example of Jesus. He is the one who can transform us, so that our minds and attitudes more and more become like his.

QUESTIONS FOR JOURNALING

1. Write about a time when you felt thoroughly loved by another person.
2. Write about a time when you loved selflessly and unreservedly.
3. How do you think relating better to God can help you love and relate better to others?

~chapter two~

LOVING
Our Family of Origin

In Charles Dickens's novel *A Christmas Carol*, Ebenezer Scrooge is carried by spirits on a transformative journey. He has to take a vivid look at his life: past, present, and future. What he sees shocks and changes him. The ghost of Christmas past shows him his past, which features greed, leading to a lost love and losing the spark in life. Each of us, like Scrooge, has a ghost of Christmas past. That ghost will haunt us until we begin to take a look at our beginnings and how they affect us now.

Growing up had been difficult for me. I was a footling breech delivered with heavy forceps. At the age of three, I had a concussion after accidentally running into a stone wall. As a result of these two incidents, even though I was very bright with words, I had difficulty with attention, keeping things in order, handwriting, and several other learning disabilities that made school an ordeal. It wasn't until I was well into adulthood that I was diagnosed with a traumatic brain injury, which accounted for my various cognitive impairments and nonverbal learning disorders.

My parents doted on me, their only child. They cherished me and wanted me, but their love was problematic at times. Without a correct diagnosis and no visible disability, my mother both didn't understand and worried about me. She thought I must be lazy and that the only way to make me act better was to shame me. She raged at me for the failings I had no control over. I felt helpless. At other times she showed affection and care. I did not know what to expect from her.

During my childhood, my dad exhibited signs of mental illness. His first episode occurred when I was five. He was hospitalized for several weeks with a diagnosis of paranoid schizophrenia. His condition was at the milder end of the spectrum and he was able to hold down a full-time job. His illness went into remission after a while, but came back in force as I entered puberty. When he was in the throes of his mental problems, he could be terrifying.

One day, I vividly remember his saying to my mother and me that he was getting a gun and would kill us. When he showed up the next day with a rifle, I managed to whisk my mother, who was near paralyzed with fear and oblivious as to what to do, out of the house. We walked to a family friend's house several blocks away where I called my Uncle Guthrie, who lived in Birmingham. He rescued us and took us back to Birmingham with him till Daddy calmed down. While we were in Birmingham, our family friends got Daddy into the hospital. He was discharged after a week and mother and I returned home.

Mother was unable to take charge. The fear had driven her into depression and anorexia. She became a skeleton from lack of eating and I was afraid I would lose her. Later, after the immediate crisis was over I heard her say to my aunt, "I wanted to escape by taking myself out, but only if I could find a way to take Eddie with me." I had been in mortal danger from both parents due to their illnesses.

My father experienced terrifying episodes for a couple or more years. When he ultimately entered remission, he turned back into a loving, nurturing father.

For most of us the past is far more than just painful memories. It also includes memories of positive relationships and all sorts of good things happening in our lives. For many of us it is an unknown jumble that significantly influences our lives here and now. Like a big submerged rock in a stream disturbs the flow of the water, so our past, particularly the parts we have not faced, changes the flow of our lives and the nature of our relationships.

How we relate to others now reflects our early relationships. Our first model of how to relate comes from our childhood experiences. Perhaps our early experiences may have had many positive loving elements that left us with strengths for loving in the here and now. In contrast, we may have grown up with put-downs from our parents rather than guidance and affirmation. Perhaps our early years were lived in a troubled home. When we have been verbally abused as children and told we are failures, as adults we can have an MP3 player in our head looping the words, "You are no good...you are a failure, a loser."

The way we relate today reflects our early home life. Dysfunctional patterns of relating often reveal a need for healing the wounds of early relationships. We human beings seem programmed to replay the past in the here and now. As William Faulkner put it, "The past is not dead! Actually, it's not even past."[5]

This chapter illustrates how opening up to the tender touch of God can aid in the healing of the past and help us recognize and overcome destructive patterns in the present. I saw this so clearly while conducting a parish retreat in the northeast over ten years ago. Mark, a relatively young man in his late thirties, asked for time alone with me. He glared at me, motionless as stone, his inner emptiness showing in his face.

At first he said nothing, just slightly turning down his jaw. Then he sighed, "I'm thinking about ending it all. Life holds little for me now."

"Tell me more," I prompted him.

"OK," he said reluctantly, "my wife has ceased loving me and I can't live without her. Nothing I do seems to help."

"How do you know this?" I asked.

His story began to come out amidst many pauses.

"Six months ago my wife Doris started work teaching high school and she has turned cold. It is as though she has left me while still remaining in the house. I loved her so much when we were younger. She is my life, my world. In our early marriage she was wonderful. She was everything I had hoped for in a woman. Now all she talks about is high school. She no longer pays attention to me. I just know she is going to leave and I'd rather be dead than see that."

As he talked more, it became apparent that the signs he thought meant his wife no longer loved him seemed little more than the normal reactions of a spouse adjusting to a new job and being gone from the house. There had to be more to it than this. I then asked him a question I usually ask when I am meeting someone for a one-time-only counseling session. "What was growing up like for you?"

He told me it was hard. His parents were both college professors. His mother lived in her head more than in her heart and was usually emotionally unavailable and distant. His father was different; he lovingly doted on his son, actively engaged in parenting, kayaked with him on weekends, and encouraged his efforts in organized sports. What nurture he had received had come from his father. When he was fourteen, however, his father's drinking exploded into full-blown alcoholism. His once-warm father grew distant. Then tragically his father was killed when he hit a bridge abutment after downing a six-pack. Mark's world was shattered.

He and Doris first fell in love their junior year in college. They agreed to marry by the beginning of their senior year. She was the most wonderful person he had ever met. He drank in her love and would grow giddy thinking she could be his. After they married Mark began to doubt her love and was always insisting that she reassure him that she cared. When she took the job teaching, Mark was sure his world was over.

As I listened to Mark, I couldn't help but wonder if he saw in her and in their relationship the distance and abandonment he experienced with his parents. I gently suggested this, but it would take much more than my telling him this for him to come to that realization himself.

Our time was limited so I reminded him that soaking in the love of God daily could help heal and rearrange our emotions and perceptions. I suggested that spiritual journaling, especially about our past, can help us open up a channel for God's healing love to give us the insight we need to heal.

I told him that I hoped he would not give up on his wife or life so easily. I suggested he start counseling meetings with the associate pastor at his parish, a licensed marriage and family therapist. I also said that it was essential to have his physician evaluate his depression and possibly put him on antidepressant medication for a time.

Two years later, when I talked to Mark again during a follow-up retreat at his parish, he was transfigured. Smiling, with Doris beside him, he told me what had happened in the intervening years. Beginning with seeing the associate pastor for counseling, he had launched into a deeper spiritual life. He rested every day in the loving silence of God's love and began journaling. He sensed an unconditional love in the center of his being, a love that would not and could not let him go. In the deep relaxation of that love, he faced his past and it became less fearsome. He had truly set his feet on a path of healing and transformation.

He realized that those euphoric times of falling in love with Doris and thinking she was the perfect person was his unconscious making her into the ideal parent he had never had. He grasped that his turning every irritable word or her preoccupation with work into her abandoning him came from the lack of trust that any real love could endure. After his perceptions cleared, his wife went to counseling with him to work on their relationship. In counseling his wife assured him of her deep love for him, but expressed her frustration that no matter what she said or did, he did not trust her love. As the prayer, counseling, and journaling went on, Mark began to trust. The two now drew close in a much deeper and solid love than the giddiness of their early days.

Psychotherapists call this replaying of the past in present relationships transference. This can be seen in psychotherapy. A client sees the therapist as the ideal person they never had growing up and falls in love with him or her. Or, just as often, the client sees the therapist as a substitute for the parent who abused and neglected them in childhood and pours a flood of hot anger on the therapist for any perceived slight. In either case the therapist, together with the client, has to work through the transference, helping to clear the client's perceptions so that the past can be past and not invade the present.

This phenomenon of transference takes place outside psychotherapy as well, in our work relationships, friendships, or with a husband or wife. A story found only in St. Mark's Gospel of Jesus healing a blind man can be used to illustrate this.

> They came to Bethsaida. Some people brought a blind man to [Jesus] and begged him to touch him. He took the blind man by the hand and led him out of the village; and when he had put saliva on his eyes and laid his hands on him, he asked him, "Can you see anything?" And the man looked up and said, "I can see people, but they look like trees, walking." Then Jesus laid his hands on his eyes again; and he looked intently and his sight was restored, and he saw everything clearly. (Mark 8:22–25)

At first, the blind man was only partially healed, seeing people as trees walking. Then Jesus laid his hands on the man's eyes and his perceptions cleared and he could see people and things the way they really were. So it is often with us—our perceptions can be fuzzy and only the touch of Jesus's hand can help us see clearly. When transference is at work, our perceptions are off. Only in the presence of an immense love, the love of God, can our perceptions clear.

Transference can even take place in our relationship with God. Perhaps we see God as the perfect parent who readily meets our needs, or a heavenly bellhop ready to do our bidding at the snap of a finger. I have seen people sour on prayer when they hold such a view. When God doesn't magically fix things in their lives, they leave prayer aside. The reality is that when prayer becomes hard it becomes more like Jesus's prayer. God wants us to walk through, not around, the shadow of death in order to find that, after all, it is just a shadow.

It is in and through the cross that we meet God. God is not a magician; instead he is the one who suffers along with us and holds us when we go through the dark valley. I remember a woman who treated God as a magician, an idealized entity who makes everything right immediately. She began to attend a prayer group at her parish. Little miracles then seemed to take place all around her. She would pray and get a good parking place. When she felt down, all she had to do was say some prayers and she was euphoric.

Then her husband was diagnosed with advanced liver cancer. She went to her prayer meeting and had everyone pray her husband would be healed. No immediate healing came. For the next month she glided along with a joy that seemed supernatural. She was filled with great hope that her husband would be healed. But as the weeks passed, no healing came and her husband's condition grew steadily worse. She felt like God had deserted her. She inwardly raged at God because things were not turning out miraculously better.

Her faith faltered. Then in further desperation she began praying before the crucifix in her church. In that simple cross she saw that God shared her suffering. For a moment she felt like she also had wounds in her hands, feet, and side. In a profound way, she saw her own wounds as the wounds her husband's illness had inflicted on both of them. After this experience her prayer turned from seeking immediate benefits from God to letting God join the suffering of his Son with hers. Her own *via dolorosa* joined with Christ's and she began sensing God in a depth she had never believed possible. This did not take away the suffering she underwent because of her husband's decline and eventual death, but it gave that suffering deep meaning. She carried a small crucifix in her purse and would at times trace the wounded figure on the cross with her fingers, letting her own pain join with Christ's. After her husband's death she walked through the hard grieving with the wounded Christ at her side. She continued in prayer and reflection throughout this time and found that God was far more than a finder of parking places. Instead, she discovered the love that turns the universe in the bosom of her soul.

Thoughtless anger can be one symptom of unresolved issues from past relationships. This is not the natural anger that rages at injustice and gives us energy to protect the helpless. It is the anger that comes from being irritated. Our angry reactions to others and the things that trigger anger in us are often symptoms of the past intruding. Whenever someone says something that ruffles us, it can set off a trigger. The easy thing to do is blame them. We think that if they changed the way they acted, everything would be all right.

The difficulty, however, is not with that person but in us. We are each responsible for our own triggers. The part of us that is wounded and in need of healing strikes back when we are triggered. The first step to healing is noticing our triggers; they help map the contours of our insecurities and lead us to the feet of a loving God who can transform those insecurities and heal those wounds. Our triggers are a cry for love, a cry for the mending of old wounds. If we look at those triggers with the eyes of faith, they provide occasion for inviting the love and compassion of God into the situation.

One of my triggers brought tension to an old and dear relationship. When Loyola Press brought out my book *Visions: The Soul's Path to the Sacred*, a prepublication version was sent to several academic and Church leaders for comment. I asked them to send copy to one of my mentors, Dr. Neely McCarter, who had taught me during my first year of theology studies and shepherded me during a rough time in my life. His comment was a sincere and solid endorsement of my book. In a separate e-mail, as a scholar and theologian, he suggested some ways the book could be improved. I took this as rejection. Blowing it all out of proportion, I shot off an angry and defensive e-mail in reply. It reached him while he was overwhelmed and busy, adding unnecessary stress to his life. When my anger subsided, I sent him another e-mail expressing regret and asking for forgiveness, which he freely gave.

My own insecurities about my performance stemmed from the learning disabilities and cognitive deficits that have plagued me all my life. Even in adulthood, even after the diagnosis of traumatic brain injury, a suggestion that my work was less than perfect could trigger a memory and shame me. Deep down I was still that terrified, fragile little boy who had struggled so much with life and school. Because I had been verbally abused as a child over my disability and told, I was "no good at all" by at least one junior high teacher, as an adult I had a loop in my mind repeating "you are no good...you are a failure, a loser, lazy, clumsy." I prayed, journaled, and talked to spiritual friends; gradually I gained the insight that while I didn't cause the abuse that left the trigger, I am one hundred percent responsible for my reactions to it and the hurt it may cause others. We all are.

When we point a finger at another, three fingers point back at us, reminding us to embrace compassion and loving-kindness, rather than accuse the other person. Martin Luther King, Jr., once said, "Love has within it a redemptive power. And there is a power there that eventually transforms."[6] When we invite the love of God into our relationships the cycle of pointing fingers is broken.

Ultimately only the medicine of God's love can take away the sting of the past. We can soak up that love in the silence of prayer. Silence is hard for many people in our society to embrace. The idea of sitting and doing nothing for a while runs counter to what our society asks us to do. We have all heard the old saying, "Don't just sit there; do something." I think what God would like to say to us is, "Don't just do something; sit there."

Before entering into the silence it might be good to take a Scripture passage and read it slowly, letting it sink into your heart. Whisper it or read it out loud; after time, you will feel the fire of God's love flame within you.

Then take time just for silence. You may wish to repeat a short prayer over and over again to anchor you in the silence. I use the Jesus Prayer, an ancient prayer of the heart in which the name of Jesus is repeated slowly. If your mind wanders, return to saying your prayer. Trying to love God *is* loving God, trying to pray *is* praying. Every time you stop praying your prayer and return to it is an act of loving God. If in the midst of a thirty-minute prayer time, wandering thoughts or sleepiness cause you to cease your prayer and you return to it a hundred times, you have made one hundred separate acts of loving God.

Let the love of God hold you in the stillness. The love that pours into you can pour out of you to your neighbor, your friends, your family, and the hurting ones of our world.

Don't worry if you fail to have feelings during your prayer. Be assured God is acting on a level in you deeper than feelings. The feelings often follow—we find that everyday reality shimmers, fresh as the first time we witnessed it; we find that the past has less of a hold.

Journaling is another way to let go of past hurts. It will call you to remember, and in that experience of remembering, you will bump into the surprising presence of God and see your past in a different light. Jeremiah, Augustine, Hildegard of Bingen, and St. Faustina are among religious figures who journaled. As we journal, the past and our own shadows become visible and ready to take to a loving God for mending.

Writing as a form of prayer does something no other form of prayer can do: it makes visible the invisible. We have lots of mental clutter, and underneath that clutter are the images, memories, stories, and thoughts that form our spiritual core. In writing, we get a chance to see the clutter, deal with it, and then draw out treasures from our core. Writing makes this inner world concrete. Our problems become visible. When we see them clearly, we can then hand them over to the God who comforts and mends. We can write about past scenes of hurt in the prayerful presence of God so often they lose their hold over us. We remember them as contents of our memory, but their emotional hold is broken.

Not only is journaling good for our souls, it's also good for our bodies. Dr. James Pennebaker, research psychologist at the University of Texas at Austin, has gathered a number of impressive studies on the effect of journal-style writing on both mental and physical health. He divided students into two groups. One group was asked to write daily on emotionally and spiritually charged topics. Another group of the same size was asked to write daily on superficial topics. The students who explored their inner life ended up having fifty percent fewer visits to the student health center than the students who wrote only on superficial topics. Laboratory tests showed wide differences in the immune systems of the groups. The results of the test on the group that journaled thoughtfully showed a measurable boost to their immune systems that remained strong long after the study.[7]

It can also be helpful to find someone to talk to about our past wounds. When someone listens to us recount our past, it grows less fearsome. We see it cease to interfere with loving others in the here and now. If the past has a deep and painful hold on us, we may need to turn to a professional listener, either a psychotherapist or a spiritual director. They can help us in moving beyond the past so that we may love others with the same love with which God loves us.

TIME FOR HEALING PRAYER
A Prayer

Dear Lord, we can love our neighbors only because you have loved us. You knew and loved us in the womb. Your love has come to us through other people. Your love comes through the waters of baptism and through touching you intimately in the Eucharist. You have loved us in your lavish forgiveness. You abide in the center of our souls, yet touch us through people, and call on us to touch others in the ways you have touched us.

Thank you for the good and wonderful parts of our pasts. Most of our lives have some joyful mysteries; times others delighted in us and nurtured us, and times we have loved others.

We also have our sorrowful mysteries; times others shamed us and belittled us, and times we looked for nurture and found an icy cold instead. May your love take away the fearsome sting of those mysteries.

Free us from the past that we may be able to reach out in love to our neighbors, family, friends, and the hurting ones who most need your love. Let the flame of your love so blaze within us that we passionately spread that love to those we meet. May your mending love help us to see people clearly and not through just the lens of the past. In you, with you, through you, reaching out to others. Amen.

SCRIPTURE TO PONDER

Read the following passages slowly, savoring each phrase, letting the words help rearrange your soul.

Before I formed you in the womb I knew you,
and before you were born I consecrated you.
(Jeremiah 1:5)

Because you have made the Lord your refuge,
the Most High your dwelling-place,
no evil shall befall you,
no scourge come near your tent.

For he will command his angels concerning you,
to guard you in all your ways.

On their hands they will bear you up,
    so that you will not dash your foot against a stone.
You will tread on the lion and the adder,
    the young lion and the serpent you will trample under
        foot.

Those who love me, I will deliver;
    I will protect those who know my name.
When they call to me, I will answer them;
    I will be with them in trouble,
    I will rescue them and honor them.
With long life I will satisfy them,
    and show them my salvation. (Psalm 91:9–16)

GUIDED MEDITATION

As you have read this chapter, painful memories from your past may have emerged. (No need to dig for them if they did not appear naturally.) Imagine that you are seated, and that Jesus takes your hand. Soft, warm relaxation flows from his body into yours, a love that slowly begins to melt away any feelings of hurt from the past. You feel the stresses of the past gather within you. Jesus shows you a large vase and tells you to leave the past's sting there. Almost as though pulling out a substance, you take the shame and hurt from your chest and stomach, and toss them into the vase. It feels so good to let go of this detritus from the past.

Then Jesus picks up the vase, embraces it, and takes it into his heart where it disappears in a living flame of love.

Then you ask Jesus, "Clear my vision that I may see people and things as they are and not through the lens of the past."

Jesus kisses each of your closed eyelids, then you open your eyes and see with sparkling clarity.

QUESTIONS FOR JOURNALING

1. Write about a time when the love of God coming directly into your heart or through another person helped remove some of the sting from past times when others may have hurt or failed you.

2. If God were to write a letter to you about some of your early experiences of being hurt, what do you think he would say? Write this out.

3. Facing the pain and shadows in our lives is fuel for compassion. As you experience God's love more and more, what are some ways you can spread this compassion to others?

~chapter three~

LOVING
Our Friends

During the painful years of my childhood, my emotions shut down. I couldn't feel the care of others. My half-Cherokee grandfather who had been my anchor, rock, and strong fortress had passed away. I had no one there for me during those years. Ice formed within me. That protective ice helped me get through the terrifying days, but it left a piercing loneliness inside of me. Awkward and clumsy because of my disability, I had not been part of the most popular set in high school. Despite the walls I built around myself, I yearned to be accepted and loved.

My first night living away from home caused me so much stress that by the next morning, my sheets were a tangled mess. I was nineteen and four hundred miles from home at Belhaven College, a Presbyterian school in Jackson, Mississippi, where I planned to begin my studies to become a Presbyterian minister. One of the reasons I chose Belhaven was because it was small and I thought I would have an easier time making friends. But I felt painfully alone that first week; several hundred other students surrounded me and I didn't know a soul. I had a prayer life, but at times even my prayer life seemed lonely. I wanted so badly to have a friend with whom I could share my soul.

In my days after arriving at Belhaven, I found many friendly people who accepted me despite my clumsiness at athletics. Still I had a yearning for something more. One night, when the loneliness grew particularly acute and the new world of college rattled me with its many demands and stresses, I was walking back to the dorm after a religious gathering. One of my new friends, Paul Evans, another pre-ministerial student, accompanied me. I heard him sigh and say, "I am being overwhelmed by school." Since I was feeling the same way, I suggested that we talk.

We decided to take a long walk through the neighborhood surrounding Belhaven. Somehow, I felt especially safe around Paul. His very posture exuded a sense of safety and acceptance. On the surface, Paul and I were different. My world was focused on the books I read rather than emotions I felt. Paul was the quintessential people person. Extroverted, athletic, and popular even in the beginning of his first year of college, he would eventually be elected president of the student body.

We both poured out all our fears, our missing of familiar surroundings, our struggles keeping up with class work, and all the challenges of living away from parents and family. When we got back to the dorm, I suggested we pray together. We climbed up the stairs to the flat roof of the dorm, tugging our Bibles along. We each read a couple of our favorite Scriptures. Mine was Matthew 11:28: "Come to me, all you that are weary and are carrying heavy burdens, and I will give you rest."

As each of us read Scripture, it seemed as though a cord of light passed from my heart to his and his to mine. We decided to meet together each evening to pray, read Scripture, and share our days. We both felt that it was not just the two of us there, but that a third was present—Christ. We became roommates. While sharing the same dorm room meant we spent more time together, we still took special time for prayer every evening, often going to the chapel on the basement floor of our dorm.

We trusted each other with the most hidden secrets of our hearts. I clearly remember the night I finally had the courage to talk about Daddy's illness and the terror it caused me growing up. He met me with acceptance. With Paul I felt an unconditional love that I hadn't experienced since my grandfather died. The only other time I had felt so loved was with a favorite high school teacher. That love helped me open my heart to let in the love of many others. Our times together enabled us to open wide our hearts with love and appreciation for everyone we met. After each of our prayer sessions we each told each other, "I love you." That's how we still close our prayer sessions and phone calls today, nearly fifty years later.

My times with Paul disposed me for the time God's love invaded me in that church in Selma. My heart was being made ready for that touch of God that eventually led me to the Catholic Church. When I started attending a Catholic parish, I had Paul's support and encouragement.

I found in my friendship with Paul a healing presence for the hurts of my past. Aelred of Rievaulx, the twelfth-century Cistercian abbot, spoke on the curative power of friendship:

> A friend is the elixir of life.... To heal the many wounds we experience in this life, no medicine is effective, powerful or truly restorative as having someone who is ready to come to us compassionately in our misfortunes and rush up to us with congratulations at every stroke of good luck.[8]

We struggled to understand the nature of our friendship. There was nothing erotic about it, nothing exclusive about it, yet it was a fountain of grace. Other students sensed our willingness to accept others, which flowed out of our mutual trust of each other. At times, they would line up outside our room to talk with us about their problems and struggles.

One night as we struggled to understand our connection, Paul pulled out his Bible and read several short passages from 1 Samuel:

> When David had finished speaking to Saul, the soul of Jonathan was bound to the soul of David, and Jonathan loved him as his own soul. (1 Samuel 18:1)

> As soon as the boy had gone, David rose from beside the stone heap and prostrated himself with his face to the ground. He bowed three times, and they kissed each other, and wept with each other; David wept the more. Then Jonathan said to David, "Go in peace, since both of us have sworn in the name of the Lord, saying, 'The Lord shall be between me and you, and between my descendants and your descendants, forever.'" He got up and left; and Jonathan went into the city. (1 Samuel 20:41–42)

Paul's heart and mine were in unison, like David and Jonathan. We invited another friend, Wil Howie, to join us. He too had a heart ready to love and accept others. The spiritual friendship of two became the spiritual friendship of three. Those sessions forever altered our three lives. Other spiritual friendships have brightened my way through the years; in particular, my friendships with Bill and Ruth Wise and Mary Timko, a friend of forty years.

After graduation and going to separate seminaries, Paul and I kept in touch. He married and took a position as Presbyterian minister in North Georgia, four hours from where I live. We often talk to each other and pray with each other over the phone. Several times a year he makes the long trip to my home in Fortson, Georgia, and we spend a day reminiscing, talking about our ministries, and praying together.

Another spiritual friendship changed the trajectory of my life. I met Robert Herrmann, another young man in my parish of St. Anne's, in the summer of 1977. At that time, my first book, *Sounds of Wonder*, had just been published and was attracting a lot of notice around the country. Robert had a marked sensitivity to the love of God. He was what I would call a natural contemplative. Like me he felt called to many hours of solitude and prayer a week. Soon after meeting our hearts drew together.

One night we felt a special urgency to pray together that we did not fully understand. Both of us lived with our parents at the time and we had nowhere to pray. We decided to pray at our parish, but the church building was closed at the time, so we decided to pray on the steps of a concrete alcove that was an entrance to the parish school. He leaned against one wall. I leaned on the opposite wall.

We prayed for a while using conversational prayer, then we entered into the silence of contemplative prayer. As I prayed, I felt God's presence like a mighty wind pass through my heart. Images of Robert and I speaking to thousands of people and basing that ministry in long and deep individual prayer and our spiritual friendship vividly shone on the movie screen of my mind.

When finished, I looked at Robert and saw his facial muscles relax into a beatific smile as words tumbled out his mouth. He described the same imagery and quiet strong wind I had experienced during our time of stillness. We had just shared an extraordinary spiritual experience. After thinking it over for the next few weeks, we decided to give it a go.

On the surface of it we were two unlikely candidates for a national ministry. We had $400 between us, but leaped ahead, renting a house to live in and use for our headquarters. The monks at Our Lady of the Holy Spirit Monastery helped shepherd us during this period. We talked our plans over with our bishop, Raymond Lessard, who put us under the guidance of the diocese. We visited Richard Rohr, O.F.M., a well-known Franciscan priest from Cincinnati, for discernment and help. He was gracious enough to come live with us for a week and help us discern our calling. He is still a great help and mentor. Our parish helped finance the ministry in our first few months. Invitations to speak on spirituality came in from all over the United States and Canada. We even gave a parish mission in Bridgetown, Barbados.

Our bishop, J. Kevin Boland, our pastor, Fr. Schreck, and our spiritual director, Fr. Doug Clark, all steered us toward the diaconate as a way of showing our solidarity with the Church in our ministry. We were ordained to the diaconate in June 2001. As part of the ceremony, we both made a promise of celibacy. Because we wanted to devote so much time to prayer and being on the road, we felt that we would not be able to be attentive to spouses and families.

In our thirty-seven years as spiritual friends, Deacon Robert and I have personally preached to over a half-million people, written eleven books, and helped form deacons in many dioceses across the country. We keep up our individual prayer and our prayer together. The love generated by our friendship has spilled over to many. Such is the power of prayerful spiritual friendship. Fr. Clark has also partnered with the two of us for shared hearts and ministry.

There are many examples of the explosive power of genuine spiritual friendships in Church history. In Scripture, the warm friendship of Ruth and her mother-in-law Naomi is a poignant example of a spiritual friendship. They made a covenant of friendship.[9] Ruth says to Naomi:

> Do not press me to leave you
>   or to turn back from following you!
> Where you go, I will go;
>   where you lodge, I will lodge;
> your people shall be my people,
>   and your God my God.
> Where you die, I will die—
>   there will I be buried.
> May the Lord do thus and so to me,
>   and more as well,
> if even death parts me from you! (Ruth 1:16–17)

Jesus shared his thoughts on friendship with his followers:

> This is my commandment, that you love one another as I have loved you. No one has greater love than this, to lay down one's life for one's friends. You are my friends if you do what I command you. I do not call you servants any longer, because the servant does not know what the master is doing; but I have called you friends, because I have made known to you everything that I have heard from my Father. (John 15:12–15)

Jesus loved his friends tenderly and compassionately while on earth. His tenderness for his follower we call "The Beloved Disciple" was the stuff of poetry. Jesus also felt special tenderness for some of his female followers, especially Martha and Mary (see John 11:5).

St. Augustine gives a personal account of the wondrous experience he and his mother shared while in Ostia waiting for a boat to Africa. In one of the most sublime passages in all of spiritual literature, Augustine described their meeting with eternity's hallowed Lover. In the villa they were using at Ostia, Augustine and his mother leaned out the window, talking pleasantly together, the garden lying before them.

> We were in the...presence of Truth...discussing together what is the nature of the eternal life of the saints: which eye has not seen, nor ear heard....We opened wide the mouth of our heart, thirsting for those heavenly streams of Your fountain...that we might be sprinkled with its waters according to our capacity.... We lifted ourselves with...ardent love.... We gradually passed through all the levels of bodily objects, and even through the heaven itself, where the sun and moon and stars shine on the earth. Indeed, we soared higher...marveling at your creation. Then with a sigh...we returned to the sounds of our own speaking.... But what is like to Your Word, our Lord, who remains...without becoming old, and 'makes all things new?[10]

St. Paulinus and his wife, Terasia, who lived in fourth-century Nola, held special spiritual and tender love for close friends like

Sulpicius Severus. Such spiritual friendships abounded during the era of the Church fathers and mothers.

The powerful grace that brightly burst out on the world among the early Franciscans was partly due to Francis's spiritual friendships with Clare, Masseo, and others. His early followers were more a band of friends than what we think of today as a religious order. These early Franciscans had a strong sense of family. God became close in the presence of friends. Francis's first biographer, Thomas of Celano, describes their sense of love for one another:

> What affection for the holy companionship of their fellows flourished among them! Whenever they came together at a place, or met along the road, and exchanged the customary greeting, there rebounded between them a dart of spiritual affection, scattering over all their devotion the seed of true love. And how they showed it! Innocent embraces, gentle tenderness, "a holy kiss," delightful converse, modest laughter, a joyous countenance, a sound eye, a humble heart, "a soothing tongue," "a mild answer," unity of purpose, a ready devotedness, and an unwearied hand to help."[11]

The Little Flowers contain the most cherished memories and traditions of Francis's early companions. One such encounter is an experience both Francis and his spiritual friend Clare shared. Francis often met with Clare to discuss spiritual matters. One day she shared a meal with Francis in front of the church of St. Mary of the Angels. Francis prepared the meal on the bare ground as he was accustomed to do. Brother Ugolino reports, "Francis began to speak of God so sweetly, so sublimely, and in a manner so wonderful, that the grace of God visited them abundantly, and all were rapt in Christ."

People nearby saw the church and the place where Clare and Francis were eating surrounded in flames. They rushed to St. Mary's to put them out. When they arrived, they found no fire. Instead they saw Francis and Clare and their companions sitting around absorbed in contemplation. Then they knew certainly, "that which they had seen was a celestial fire, not a material one, which God miraculously had sent to bear witness to the divine flame of love." The people returned home, after witnessing this sacred moment "with great consolation in their hearts."[12]

Friendships between male and female celibates were common. In addition to Clare and Francis, St. Francis de Sales and St. Jeanne de Chantal also shared a close bond as did Blessed Jordan of Saxony, the successor to St. Dominic, and a Dominican nun, Blessed Diana of Andalo. Blessed Jordan wrote in a letter to Diana:

> The longer we are separated from each other the greater becomes our desire to see one another again…. Yet whatever we may write matters little, beloved: within our hearts is the ardor of our love in the Lord whereby you speak to me and I to you continuously in those wordless outpourings of charity which no tongue can express nor letter contain.[13]

The pinnacle of writing on spiritual friendship came with Aelred of Rievaulx, a twelfth-century Cistercian abbot. His book *Spiritual Friendship* is as apropos now as it was nine centuries ago. He says that knowing a friend deeply can help us know Christ. For him the closeness of friends helps us to embrace God: "In this way, beginning with the love with which he has embraced his friend, and rising up to the love with Christ, he will with great happiness enjoy the delight of the friendship of friendships (i.e., friendship with God)."[14]

Originally written for monks, his ideas on friendship give great wisdom for friendships outside the cloister. It's a book that can help anyone seeking help in relationships. For Aelred, spiritual friendships usually start from more ordinary friendships, and then grow into deeper relationships.

Spiritual friendships, all good friendships for that matter, don't just happen; they take time and energy to build. Two acquaintances don't just decide to become spiritual friends. It is something that emerges from more ordinary, everyday friendship. Spiritual friendships come about when two people are each on a journey to God and share their mutual journeys. While it is not necessary to pray together every day, it is important to talk about God and the spiritual life together.

Spiritual friendships respect each person's independence. We don't try to fit the other person into our idea of what they should be and do. Rather than merge, friends respect each other's uniqueness. Open communication is also a necessity. Friends grow to trust each other and become vulnerable to each other. They trust each another with the secrets of their hearts.

Like any good relationship, spiritual friendships should be generative. As friends together they should reach out to others with love. I remember a deeply devout married couple who wanted spiritual friends in order to enhance their marriage and bring greater fulfillment to their own relationship. They never found what they were looking for because they were not looking to give their hearts away in service and love to others.

Friends are quick to forgive: both to ask for forgiveness and to give forgiveness. Even the best of friendships can have stormy times. They survive these difficult patches through the kind of commitment that outlasts temporary pain and failure to communicate. Spiritual friends are committed for the long haul.

Ideally, for Christians, marriage should also be a spiritual friendship. Couples can include God and prayer in their relationship. They can share the deep reaches of their souls with each other. They can take a mighty journey to God and with God, both individually and together.

I met Jim and Marie on a parish mission. Jim was the spiritual life coordinator for their parish and had invited Deacon Robert and me to speak. Together, this couple exuded calm and tenderness that enveloped those near them in a cloud of peace and safety. Several years earlier, their three-year-old daughter, their only child, had died of a quickly progressing cancer and, rather than properly grieve their losses, they passed guilt back and forth between them like a hot potato. Jim stopped talking to Marie because it hurt so much to talk about their lost daughter. Both began to fly off the handle with each other at the slightest provocation. Something had to change.

They still attended church but both found it difficult. Marie especially could not understand how a loving God could take their daughter away. In the face of such loss, they watched their marriage begin to shatter. Jim could not feel the presence of God emotionally, but he knew somehow that only God could take them through the tough times and salvage their marriage.

He made a two-week silent retreat at a nearby monastery. In the raw silence of those two weeks, he had to face his loss. In almost a spiritual agony in that first week, he felt the holy silence begin to hollow out a place in his soul for God. He turned to the Scriptures, particularly Jeremiah, "I have loved you with an everlasting love" (Jeremiah 31:3). As he softly repeated that passage he felt the gentle breeze of God's love blow through him body and soul. Now, he wept not just for his daughter and his failing marriage, but because God loved him so tenderly. He still grieved hard for his daughter and on some level always will, but he now knew he walked through that dark valley, not alone, but with God beside him to catch his tears.

When Jim returned home, the deep down peace that filled him helped him respond to his wife's rage with heartfelt understanding. Once when his wife lunged into him verbally, rather than strike back, as he had been accustomed to do before the retreat, he instead enfolded her in his arms, began weeping and said to her, "It has been so hard, hasn't it, so hard."

Marie began to weep too, returning the embrace and saying, "It is hard, isn't it?"

As one, they moved toward the couch, knelt, held hands, and began praying together.

What happened that day was the beginning of the healing of their marriage and the birth of a wonderful spiritual friendship. They began seeing a grief counselor together. They knelt and prayed every day. Marie also made a retreat that launched her into contemplative spirituality. Gradually, rich compassion for others began to flow from their spiritual friendship. People could sense God just by being in their presence. They became involved with their parish and with Cursillo, a movement of conversion of heart. A fountain of goodness poured forth from their love of each other and their shared love of God.

We can also experience this kind of spiritual friendship with other family members. Despite my father's mental illness when I was little, our hearts drew near as the years passed. My father and I had never been as close as we were the last few weeks of his life. Knowing that we might not have too long together, I had been going over to my parents' house to record his early memories to pass on to my larger family. He talked about the things most sacred to him: God, the memories of his Native American grandmother who taught him to hunt with stone-tipped arrows, and how much he cherished me and my mother.

I had always loved him and he had always loved me, but we began to relate on deeper and deeper spiritual levels we had not imagined possible before. There were many times I felt the tender spiritual presence that was my father as I went about my daily work. Part of my heart glowed with the light of his presence, even though he lived twenty miles away. Even with him physically away from me his presence in my heart delighted my soul. He said he felt my presence in the same way. What we experienced is what Aelred of Rievaulx called a spiritual kiss that two souls united in Christ can feel.

> No medicine is more valuable than a friend. He will be someone whose soul will be to us a refuge to creep into when the world is altogether too much for us, and someone to whom we can confide all our thoughts. His spirit will give us the comforting kiss that heals all the sickness of our preoccupied hearts. He will weep with us when we are troubled, and rejoice when we are happy. He will always be there to consult when we are in doubt. And we will be so deeply bound to him in our hearts that

even when he is far away we shall find him together with us in spirit.[15]

At eighty-five, he took ill the Friday before Easter 1996. His symptoms included lots of abdominal pain, vomiting, and high blood pressure. By Saturday he perked up and was feeling much better. I talked to him Sunday night and, despite a touch of dementia, his voice conveyed his usual love and gentleness. I told him he was the best father in the world. The news came Monday morning that he had died of a massive heart attack.

Time for Healing Prayer
A Prayer

Dear Lord, you have been a friend to each of us. In creation you called the entire cosmos into friendship. In Jesus's friends you gave us a model of friendship. By becoming one with us in the incarnation you offered eternal friendship to each of us, your children. You have called us into friendship with one another. May we befriend others with the same love with which you befriended humankind.

Lead us into spiritual friendships gently and gradually. Help us to commit to others just as you committed yourself to us. Help keep our love for one another pure and life giving. Lord, help us to allow your love, the one love, to be the same love with which we love one another, and the same love with which we reach out to a hurting world.

Scripture to Ponder

If I speak in the tongues of mortals and of angels, but do not have love, I am a noisy gong or a clanging cymbal. And if I have prophetic powers, and understand all mysteries and all knowledge, and if I have all faith, so as to remove mountains, but do not have love, I am nothing. If I give away all my possessions, and if I hand over my body so that I may boast,* but do not have love, I gain nothing.

Love is patient; love is kind; love is not envious or boastful or arrogant or rude. It does not insist on its own way; it is not irritable or resentful; it does not rejoice in wrongdoing, but rejoices in the truth. It bears all things, believes all things, hopes all things, endures all things.

Love never ends. But as for prophecies, they will come to an end; as for tongues, they will cease; as for knowledge, it will come to an end. For we know only in part, and we prophesy only in part; but when the complete comes, the partial will come to an end. When I was a child, I spoke like a child, I thought like a child, I reasoned like a child; when I became an adult, I put an end to childish ways. For now we see in a mirror, dimly, but then we will see face to face. Now I know only in part; then I will know fully, even as I have been fully known. And now faith, hope, and love abide, these three; and the greatest of these is love. (1 Corinthians 13:1–13)

Guided Meditation

Begin to slow down. Put on some soothing music and begin to drift slowly into the depth of comfort God offers everyone. Rest, still and quiet, in his presence. In the moving picture that is memory, recall some of your early healthy friendships as a child and young adult. Feel the joy again; remember the oneness you felt with friends.

If in remembering the good times you also recalled painful times with friends, think of one or more scenes of pain. Now, picture Jesus entering the scene, embracing you, and saying, "My love can make up for the early pains of life."

Think of your current sets of relationships with both friends and relatives. See scenes from those friendships. Is there joy in those relationships? Now see in your mind's eye what you can do to enhance those friendships.

Now picture where you are seated, and a fountain flowing upward in your body spilling out the love of God, the source of the fountain, on all your friends. Finally, picture the love you share with friends expand and cover the whole world, especially touching the neediest, the sick, prisoners, and outcasts, causing the whole globe of the earth to glow with the love of God that powers your friendships.

QUESTIONS FOR JOURNALING

1. What are some of the things you can do to enhance your relationships with friends or your spouse?

2. Are there times you felt God come to you through friends? Write about them.

3. Are some of your friendships ready to become spiritual friendships? If so, what can you do to help that transition?

~chapter four~

LOVING
Our Family

A generation ago Fr. Patrick Peyton, C.S.C., in his push for family prayer, coined the phrase, "The family that prays together, stays together." This is backed up by statistics. Regular attendance at religious services is linked to healthy, stable family life, strong marriages, and well-behaved children. The practice of religion also leads to a reduction in the incidence of domestic abuse, crime, substance abuse, and addiction. In addition, religious practice leads to an increase in physical and mental health, longevity, and education attainment. Moreover, these effects are intergenerational, as grandparents and parents pass on the benefits to the next generations.[16]

Few things draw families closer than shared devotions. In prayer the focus turns outward toward a higher reality. It is as though a cord of light flows from the heart of each family member to the other, binding the family together. Gregory and Suzanne Wolfe, authors of a book on family devotions, put it this way, "Prayer can help everyone—children and grown-ups alike—close the gap between the sacred and the ordinary, evoking a deeper sense of gratitude, love, and intimacy."[17]

Family prayer can start each parent and each child on a powerful spiritual journey.

Pediatrician Dr. William Sears and his wife, Martha, write in their book *The Successful Child*: "Many parents devote a great deal of effort to shaping their child's intellectual, emotional or physical development, but they shy away from teaching spirituality. They are neglecting a critical tool for success. Prayer also makes belief more real and shapes the identity of a family." Family prayer "teaches empathy," they say, "especially as siblings pray for each other."[18]

Family prayer becomes a window for children on their parents' experience of God. By sharing their needs in prayer, parents become vulnerable to their children and this encourages children to open up their hearts to their siblings and one another, fostering a tender emotional and spiritual closeness.

Family prayer does more than create transparency and intimacy, it gives our family roots. I read the story of a man who lived through a tornado touching down a hundred feet from his house. After the sound and fury of the storm had passed, he saw that the pine trees on his land had been uprooted by the storm. In that part of the country they had shallow roots. The big, tall oak tree on his land had lost some leaves but was otherwise intact. The difference was the roots. Unlike the pines, the oak tree had elaborate and deep roots and was able to weather even a tornado. Marriages and families who put down roots can remain intact in the midst of life's many storms.

In families headed by a married couple, that means the husband and wife deepen their relationship by putting down strong spiritual roots through praying together, frequenting the sacraments, and fostering compassion. This rootedness can be passed on to the children through family devotions and God-filled parenting.

This truth is found in these words from John 15:4–5: "Abide in me as I abide in you. Just as the branch cannot bear fruit by itself unless it abides in the vine, neither can you unless you abide in me. I am the vine, you are the branches. Those who abide in me and I in them bear much fruit, because apart from me you can do nothing."

The first essential of putting down roots means a daily experience of God through prayer and sacrament. Prayer is an essential component. Communicating with God through conversation and silence greatly deepens parents' roots as well as children's roots.

Through the ages certain disciplines and experiences root us as Christians. One of those is daily prayer. St. Paul tells us in Philippians 4:6–7, "Do not worry about anything, but in everything by prayer and supplication with thanksgiving let your requests be made known to God. And the peace of God, which surpasses all understanding, will guard your hearts and your minds in Christ Jesus."

Another essential in developing roots is daily Scripture reading. Scripture is the owner's manual for the spiritual life. A good habit is reading the daily readings for Mass. Scripture can become far more than words that offer information. Scripture, if we pray it as well as read it, can burrow deep in our unconscious, plunging deep down in our souls.

Writer Ken Locke was brought up in a family that had regular family devotions. "From the time my brother and I were born until we moved away from home," he remembers, "we participated in family devotions." His father would begin each day by calling the family together for Scripture reading, devotional reading, and prayer. If there were guests staying with them, they too were invited.

Everyone in the family took turns reading and praying. "Often we would spend a few extra minutes to discuss what we had read," Ken says, "and how it could be applied to that day's events." Ken has never forgotten these mornings. Not only were they together as a family every day, but they grew spiritually from their reading and their prayers. "Many of the Bible verses and devotional illustrations have stuck in my mind," Ken reflects, "that no matter how far I may stray from God, some memory from those mornings always helps to bring me back."

Years later Ken realizes that his parents taught him the importance of being together as a family. But more important, they taught him the importance of "family worship and about happiness and guidance that come from the daily study of scripture."[19]

Another rooting experience is worship. As often as possible, frequent the Eucharistic celebration. In the Eucharist we physically experience the depths of God. If a couple has the time, using morning or evening prayer from the Liturgy of the Hours joins the marriage prayer with the prayer of the Church.

In two-parent families, the couple spends time enriching and deepening their relationship with each other. Couple prayer is essential for this. Couple closeness involves more than the two parents; it involves God. Marriage is a three-way relationship. As Dennis and Barbara Rainey put it in their book *Growing Spiritually Strong Families*, "Since [God] is so intimately involved wouldn't it be natural for God to desire that couples bring their needs and praises to God on a daily basis."[20] Few things will enhance families more than the married couple taking time for conversational prayer each day.

Not every family is headed by a couple. It is necessary for the single parent to develop strong peer relationships through spiritual friendship and bonding with other adults, such as grown siblings and the single parent's own parents.

Couples and families can talk to God; God can talk to couples and families. This assurance is at the heart of conversational prayer, an intimate communication between friends. Jesus listens to us; we listen to him. Hardly anything comforts and eases us more than someone who lovingly listens. Jesus—the greatest listener, the greatest friend—experienced our fears, our stresses, and our worries. He understands us more than anyone. Alphonsus de Liguori, the patron saint of conversational prayer, lived in Italy during the eighteenth century. In his book, *Prayer as Conversing with God as a Friend*, he wrote, "God's heart has no greater concern than to love us and to make itself loved by us" This is the core principle of conversational prayer. He continues, "Always act toward God like faithful friends who consult with each other on everything…Accustom yourself to speak to God, one-to-one, in a familiar manner as to the dearest friend you have and who loves you best of all." Not only do we speak with God in conversational prayer, God speaks to us: "God will not make himself heard by you in a voice that reaches your ears but rather in a voice that only your heart knows well.[21]

Any prayer in which you converse personally with God can be called conversational prayer. Rosalind Rinker, a former Protestant missionary to China, has written a score of books on conversational prayer, and has led hundreds of experiential workshops on the subject. She worked closely with the Catholic bishop of Little Rock in teaching conversational prayer throughout his diocese. Her work influenced the widely used Catholic Bible study called the Little Rock Bible Study. As much as possible, she urges people to pray out loud as they converse with God. I have found speaking the words just under my breath, moving tongue and lips a little, physically reinforces the prayer and works just as well. (Some people write out their conversational prayers.) The following steps of prayer were drawn from Rosalind Rinkers's four steps of conversational prayer.

> *Jesus is here.* Recognize the Risen Lord's nearness. Welcome Him out loud or silently in your own words. I often pray: "You are so near me, Lord, closer to me than my breath. Please open Your listening heart to my prayers."
>
> *Thank You, Lord.* Think over all the ways Jesus has loved and cared for you. Name some of those times, and thank Him for them. Offer praise, worship and adoration.
>
> *Help me, Lord.* We take our needs to Jesus one by one. We tell Him about our cares, admit our sins, and ask Him for guidance.
>
> *I pray for my brothers and sisters.* We move beyond ourselves to pray for others. We think of their needs, their cares. We pray for this hurting world of ours. We open our hearts wide in compassion.[22]

Making time for silence is one of the most important things families can do. In the stillness, our hearts are knit with God's and with one another's.

One family I know personally began to consciously cultivate silence at family devotions. Besides the parents, the family
consisted of a fourteen-year-old son, an eleven-year-old daughter,
and an eight-year-old son. After a sacred text was read and each
family member had a chance to pray out loud, a candle would be
lit and the family would sit in silent prayer for five or six minutes.
In those silences, God who comes in the stillness too deep for
words tied their hearts together. After the silence, each member
of the family had a chance to say in a sentence or two what was
on their hearts. Simple and profound words would pour forth. In
one case, after the silence, the mother who had lost her temper
early in the day simply said a heartfelt, "Please forgive me." Other
times members would say, "It's been a good day" or "God is good
to us." The silent time and the words that came after profoundly
bound the family together. Group silence reminds us that the
experience of God is not so much taught as caught.

Couple prayer can begin with one partner reading a short
Scripture, perhaps taken from the reading of the day. Then
perhaps follow Rinker's outline for conversational prayer. Each
partner can take time praying. In family prayer, invite the children, no matter what their age, to say some prayers.

TIME FOR HEALING PRAYER
A Prayer

Dear Jesus, thank you for the gift of family, for the domestic
Church. Above all else, as a family help us to center our lives
around the beating heart of your love. You are the one in the
midst of our family who gives us eternal roots.

You were born into a family with Joseph and Mary. In your
incarnation you took all of humankind as your family. You have

passed on to us the triune love that is at the heart of reality. Because of you, all humankind is family.

Help our particular family here on earth to take time to center on you, to let you be the healer and redeemer in the midst of family.

There have been so many times we have failed at being compassionate with one another. Help us, through your understanding, compassion, and boundless empathy to show compassion and empathy for one another. Amen.

SCRIPTURE TO PONDER

Abide in me as I abide in you. Just as the branch cannot bear fruit by itself unless it abides in the vine, neither can you unless you abide in me. I am the vine, you are the branches. Those who abide in me and I in them bear much fruit, because apart from me you can do nothing. (John 15:4–5)

Rejoice in the Lord always; again I will say, Rejoice. Let your gentleness be known to everyone. The Lord is near. Do not worry about anything, but in everything by prayer and supplication with thanksgiving let your requests be made known to God. And the peace of God, which surpasses all understanding, will guard your hearts and your minds in Christ Jesus. (Philippians 4:4–7)

Then little children were being brought to him in order that he might lay his hands on them and pray. The disciples spoke sternly to those who brought them; but Jesus said, "Let the little children come to me, and do not stop them; for it is to such as these that the kingdom of heaven belongs." And he laid his hands on them and went on his way. (Matthew 19:13–15)

GUIDED MEDITATION

Take time to be still. Perhaps say the Jesus Prayer. Let the love of God pour over you. Rest in the calm awhile. You find yourself and your family walking in along a rocky path in another place, another time.

It's early morning, just a moment before the sun rises. You turn a corner and come to a tomb with the stone rolled away. Light pours from the empty tomb. Suspended in the air at the entrance of the tomb is Jesus, his face bright with joy. His arms are outstretched, and you can see the wounds the nails made in his hands and feet. You see the wound the spear made in his side. Brilliant light shines from each wound.

You stand still, looking at Jesus as he looks at you. The light that encircles him now enfolds you and your family. The light caresses you, nurtures you, and warms you, as it brings great joy. You breathe in the light. It fills your lungs. The light surrounds your blood cells until—inside and out—you are saturated with the light. This is the light of Christ, the light that remakes the world. That light now remakes you and brings you to fresh life.

Rest a moment in the light. As you look at Jesus, talk to him.

First thank him. Thank him for all the ways his love has helped you.

Next, tell him your family's needs. Tell him about the ways you need his help in your life.

Now tell him about other people and situations that need his help. Pray for peace and justice. Pray that human life be respected and protected from the moment of conception till the moment of natural death. See the whole world surrounded and embraced by the light of Christ, which streams from his empty tomb.

Gently return to this time and rest in the stillness as the light of Christ surrounds your whole family.

QUESTIONS FOR JOURNALING

1. Think of some times you engaged in the dialogue with God we call conversational prayer. What was it like? What were the feelings it gave you?
2. Envision your family praying together. What is it like?
3. If you are married, how much of God do you encounter with your spouse?

~chapter five~

LOVING
Our Coworkers

Many of us spend forty to sixty hours a week working. If we include our volunteer work, we find that the majority of our time awake is spent in the workplace. We know God needs to be not just in our prayer times and hours spent in church or with family, but in the many hours we spend at work. Yet, it can be easy to build a wall between work and the rest of our lives. But we don't wave goodbye to God when we enter the workplace. We need to take him with us.

Scripture illustrates that God is present in the midst of the work-place. Amos was a farmer. David was a shepherd. Abraham was one of most successful entrepreneurs of his time. Peter, James, and John were fishermen; Matthew, a tax collector. Luke may have been a physician, and Paul tells us that he worked as a tentmaker.

Perhaps you work in a cubicle with a phone, or alone in a toll booth every day, handing out change. Work may involve a computer in the home or a smartphone or tablet in your hand that connects you with the office and the world. Regardless of where you work or what you do, every position is rooted in relationship. Every job touches the lives of others.

Let's face it: Today's workplace can be a pressure cooker. The hustle and bustle, the personality clashes, and many other aspects of work can turn the workplace into a near toxic environment. Having a prayer life, using meditation, memory, and imagination, can all enable us to have a fruitful time at work. Christ said, "Love your neighbor." That certainly includes our fellow workers. If we go into work with hearts schooled in compassion we can subtly help change the atmosphere at work.

Prayer is indeed a school of compassion. It is easy for us to live on a physical or an intellectual level in our relationships at work, but we often miss the intuitive, subconscious cues that come to us. Imagination helps us transcend these problems and overcome our separateness.

My friend Bill used his imagination to help heal relationships at work. In one instance, his relationship with his boss was strained. What was once a close friendship was deteriorating. His boss continually belittled him, and Bill reacted defensively. Cold anger consumed him. Spontaneity disappeared from their friendship and their work suffered.

Bill took a lunch hour to go to a nearby chapel where he could relax and pray. In his imagination he went into the boss's office, looked him in the eye, and said, "John, what's the problem?" His boss broke down, cried and said, "I'm not going to go any further in this company. My life seems over. My youth and vitality and potential are all wasted. I'm lonely." These words broke Bill's heart open. He realized that his boss felt like a failure and was crying out for affirmation and compassion.

The next day Bill was met with many of the same belittling comments, but he could look past those to the hurt that caused them. He began to experience heartfelt compassion and sensitivity for his boss. His prayer session had helped him become aware of subconscious intuitive signals. He got to the heart of the problem and now reacted with affirmation. His attitude began to change his boss. The boss slowly stopped his belittling comments. The two began to have many heart-to-heart talks. The relationship blossomed and became even more spontaneous and alive than before.

Taking time in your prayer period to recall interactions with people during the workday and give them to God is a daily discipline that can spill out in more compassionate, sensitive treatment of fellow workers, customers, and/or clients.

Another way to bring meaning to work is to seek God's help in overcoming the stress of work so that we can do the finest work possible. Finding time for silence during the bustle of the work day can be hard but rewarding. One woman I know uses her long commute to work to say the rosary, using a little rosary ring she always carries in her purse. Another worker may carry lunch to work, rather than going out, and uses the saved time for solitude and reflection.

Doing work of quality can be viewed as one of the most spiritual things we can do. As the Rev. Martin Luther King, Jr. said: "If a man is called to be a street sweeper, he should sweep streets even as Michelangelo painted or Beethoven composed music. He should sweep streets so well that all the host of heaven and earth will pause to say, 'There lived a great street sweeper who did his job well.'"[23]

Marianne E. Roche, in *On-The-Job Spirituality: Finding God in Work*, writes, "It is who we are and how we are when we are working that is the measure for the real value of our work, both to us and to others."[24] A corporate attorney, Catholic, and holder of a master's degree in religion, Roche says work can be a sacrament. "Work is a gift from God…. Our work is a means to communicate or effect the love and presence of God in our midst."[25]

"Spirituality is not about bringing religion into the workplace," Gregory Pierce says in *Spirituality at Work*. "It's about raising awareness of the deeper meaning of what you're doing in your job." Pierce suggests we try this definition of work: "Work is all the effort (paid or unpaid) we exert to make the world a better place, a little closer to the way God would have things."[26]

Some people think bringing religion to work means trying to proselytize others in order to convince them one's religion is the true path, or attempt to get them to have a particular religious experience. The ideal is to let our faith, our religion, so change our hearts that we become sensitive, caring people with both coworkers and customers. We do not need so much to argue someone into faith, but so saturate ourselves in the One Love that turns the universe so that our very personality exudes God's presence.

The workplace should be a place where people discover meaning and purpose in their work. Ideally, it should be a place where faith stories can be shared. However, the shadow side of sharing faith is proselytizing, pushing one's own brand of religion and trying to impose faith on others.

Diane was an administrative assistant at the headquarters of a large manufacturing business. She worked for the head of the company's sales division, Mr. Johnson. She also helped coordinate the work of several sales associates. As a result, she rubbed elbows with many people at her job.

A Catholic, she had recently rediscovered her Church after a fifteen-year absence. She had explored apologetic websites that sought to prove that Catholicism was right and other faith expressions were wrong or at least defective. This rekindled her faith and brought her back to the Catholicism of her youth. She wanted to share her newfound faith with colleagues and customers alike. Wanting to make her desk a Catholic space, she put a stand-up crucifix there as well as a "Pray the Rosary" bumper sticker on the side of her desk. She rejoiced that her boss was Catholic and chairman of the spirituality and adult formation committee at his own parish. From all she had heard, he was a good, caring executive, cherishing the employees under him, and seeking the ideas and input of all those in his division.

Soon after her return to the Church, Diane kept trying to argue with her coworkers, some Jewish, some Protestant, about the truth of the Catholic faith. Her zeal created tension in the workplace. She asked her boss to pray a decade of the rosary with her and any other Catholics she could stir up at work. He immediately gave her an unadorned, "No," and then commented that he had had several complaints about her pushing her religion—"It gets on people's nerves."

Diane left his office in tears. She couldn't understand why such a devout Catholic as her boss could be so negative about saying the rosary. His no to her was an unambiguous sign that in his mind, she was going too far in pushing her Catholicism.

An hour later he summoned her back into his office. Diane feared the worst, that she was being terminated.

When she entered his office the warm smile on his face dispelled her worst fears.

"Sit down," he told her. "Can I pour you some coffee?" She nodded yes and he poured coffee for the two of them.

"Please forgive me for my harshness earlier," he said. "I understand your coming back to the Church was a pivotal experience for you. Tell me about it."

She swallowed hard and kept her telling of her return to the Church concise. She felt a peace come over her. He was really listening to her. In a calm and assured tone, Mr. Johnson said, "I rejoice with you in your rediscovery of God and the Church. I have felt close to the Church all my adult life. Like you, I love the rosary. In fact, I say the rosary on my long drive to work every day. I pray for my coworkers, my department, and the whole company. I ask each day that I may be an instrument of his peace. I don't succeed in being that instrument as often as I would like, but I do find my private time with God every day schools my heart in the deep rich peace that his presence brings.

"My concern for you is not that you relish your Catholicism, but that you seem to try to push it onto others. I can't help but wonder if it is not yourself you are trying to persuade into belief by arguing your case to others. We should pray the rosary not so much to get others to say the rosary as to let the prayers comfort and change us in the deep interior of our souls. When we pray that way we can become emblems, touch points of the peace God brings us.

"I notice your parish is named 'St. Francis of Assisi.' I remember hearing someone quote a saying of Francis, 'Preach the Gospel at all times, and only use words if necessary.' We need to let the Gospel form us and change us. That way we can convey God's presence because his peace floods our interior like a spring and pours out of us like a fountain with all we meet.

"I don't mean to sound preachy, but I do think the best course for you is to actually taste the goodness of God, not to lean on arguments and ideas you believe prove God and prove the faith. My own parish is having a retreat at the end of the month on how to experience God. It is much more a matter of tasting God than telling about God."

These were strong words, but Diane said she was touched as well as challenged by them, because they were spoken with profound calm and kindness.

Diane made the retreat her boss suggested, joined a faith sharing small group at her own parish, and slowly she began to fall in love with God, rather than just arguing ideas about God. She took down her crucifix at work and became a more compassionate listener to her coworkers rather than simply a promoter of the Church.

Tensions eased and her fellow workers began to warm and sense a new peace about her. A few felt free enough to tell her about their own spiritual journeys. Ultimately, Diane found great meaning at work.

For those of us involved in Church ministry, keeping the focus on God-centered relationships is even more important. No matter what our churches are focused on, without love, they are as Paul puts it "a noisy gong or a clanging cymbal" (1 Corinthians 13:1). Without love our parishes become noisemakers; empty and discordant. Without love churches repel people; with love they tenderly shepherd them as a good shepherd cares for the lambs. Believers are hungry, not for intricate debates, or even culture wars, but for presence, the raw and tender presence of God. We can radiate that presence only if we open ourselves to a loving God and share that love with others. Faith is to be lived, not fought over.

It is so easy in today's society for Church staffs to use a business model to define themselves: being efficient and getting the work done no matter what. Several months ago I talked to different classes in a school at a parish where Deacon Robert and I were conducting a parish mission. The seventh-grade class seemed lively and full of energy. When Deacon Robert asked them, "Have any of you experienced stress before?" all hands went up and many glanced at their teacher.

"The way we handle it is to have the whole class take five minutes before each class for silent prayer," one student volunteered.

Those students had their hearts in the right place; prayer can ease our stresses and our fears. In full-time Church work, private prayer can calm us, helping us to be kind to those we work with and greet everyone we meet with kindness.

Another important element in Church work is to have a daily staff prayer time as well as staff retreats every few months or so.

I remember giving an afternoon retreat to a large parish staff in the South. They did not usually have regular prayer times together or retreats. I was scheduled to meet with them on the parish grounds from 1 P.M. to 4 P.M., after a regular morning work day. When everyone arrived in the meeting room, faces were blank or fidgety. It was obvious they didn't want to be there. I heard one staff member whisper to another, "I hope this doesn't last long; I'd like to get home early for a change." Furthermore it appeared to me that the staff members, while polite with each other, were not friendly with each other. There was a whiff of tension in the air. I knew my ability to help the group was limited. God would have to do the heavy lifting.

First of all, I led them in a session of quiet prayer, using the "Going Home" section of Dvorak's *New World Symphony* as background music, and having them silently whisper the name of Jesus over and over again to anchor them in the silence.

Ease came over their faces as they rested silently together in the love of God. Tension fled from the room, replaced by peacefulness.

After that first prayer experience I asked them to write about the time God touched them. Then I asked those who were willing to share their stories with the group.

One of the secretaries wrote about the time she felt the warmth of God's comfort a week after the death of her husband. The principal of the school told of a time he was hiking and camping in the mountains and was overcome by the beauty he saw. The Director of Religious Education told of how AA had helped her to sobriety and how she found God in her fellow strugglers at AA meetings. Each person on the staff had uncovered a sacred part of their soul for others to see. All had listened intently as each person spoke.

We went through several more prayer exercises and sharing afterward. To finish, I had each person talk about their experience of the afternoon of prayer. Most everyone remarked how much closer they felt after telling others a part of their own spiritual journey. The pastor said he had never felt closer to his fellow staff members. The consensus was that this was the first time they had related to one another on the heart level rather than just processing work together.

At the pastoral associate's suggestion, they began praying together weekly as a staff and started taking monthly afternoon retreats. The newfound closeness of the staff spread throughout the parish and the school until the parish more resembled a family than an institution.

Another discipline to cultivate in the Church workplace is to live with ambiguity and imperfection, in oneself and others. Especially because Church staffs are expected to be more Christlike than secular workplace staffs, each staff member can expect too much from other staff members. Plus, regular members of the parish can expect much more of the staff.

God doesn't expect us to do everything perfectly. He just asks that we depend on him. Soon after I was ordained and started leading parish missions across the country, I keenly felt my inadequacies. If an audience did not have tears in their eyes after a presentation I gave and praise it afterward, telling me it was wonderful, I felt like I had failed and beat up on myself. This bore down on me and made me nervous. Feeling like I wasn't doing my best kept me, at times, from actually doing my best.

I took this to a priest in the sacrament of reconciliation and he reminded me that we all hold the treasure of God's love and presence in earthly vessels. God wanted me to realize, that I, of my own power, did not have the ability to touch and heal others; that was the work of the Holy Spirit. All I was called to do was prepare and trust God to move among the audience in his own time and way. The priest told me, "God loves you, Eddie, when you make mistakes and are worried or anxious. Don't so much trust in your skills and talents as his tender mercies."

When he finished I remembered a story from an Episcopal priest, Fr. Jeff. He said there was a middle-aged man in his Church that seemed to never be listening or moved by the Mass or sermon.

One Sunday as he greeted the man after Mass, he smiled broadly at the priest and met him with a firm and warm handshake saying that the sermon had truly spoken to him.

"What did I say that so touched you?" Fr. Jeff asked, anticipating it must have been something profound he said.

The man replied, "It was when you said, 'Now let's move from the first half of the sermon to the second half.' I realized I now must move from the first half to the second half of my life."

As Church workers, we do the best we can do within our human limitations and trust God to do the healing and touching of the people we encounter.

Another thing we can do in our Church work is learn to accept and forgive the foibles and imperfections of others. Like us they are human and have our individual challenges. Hearts ready to forgive and ask forgiveness are essential in Church work.

Showing gratitude and appreciation for others is essential in Church work, or any other work for that matter. Affirm others and remember to thank them for their services.

TIME FOR HEALING PRAYER
A Prayer

Dear Lord, you call us, your children, to work. Work gives great meaning in our lives, knits us together with fellow workers, and schools us to become more caring. When you were among us here on earth, you both preached and lived the kingdom, forming close ties with your disciples, your fellow workers. In your work you healed, you taught, and formed strong bonds with others. You taught us compassion by incarnating the compassion and One Love that beats at the very center of life.

Help us gently, with the aid of your Spirit, to do your work in the world. Help us walk so closely with you, so that when we touch others in our work we become a channel for your touch. Teach us to accept our imperfections and go to you at every turn. Amen.

SCRIPTURE TO PONDER

After this the Lord appointed seventy others and sent them on ahead of him in pairs to every town and place where he himself intended to go. He said to them, "The harvest is plentiful, but the laborers are few; therefore ask the Lord of the harvest to send out laborers into his harvest. Go on your way. See, I am sending you out like lambs into the midst of wolves. Carry no purse, no bag, no sandals; and greet no one on the road. Whatever house you enter, first say, 'Peace to this house!' And if anyone is there who shares in peace, your peace will rest on that person; but if not, it will return to you. Remain in the same house, eating and drinking whatever they provide, for the laborer deserves to be paid. Do not move about from house to house. Whenever you enter a town and its people welcome you, eat what is set before you; cure the sick who are there, and say to them, 'The kingdom of God has come near to you.'" (Luke 10:1–9)

GUIDED MEDITATION

Notice your breathing. Let each breath be a prayer that eases you deeper into the quiet of God. Rest in God's presence a few moments. Imagine your workplace and the different people who are there. In your imagination, go to several coworkers and ask, "What is your life like right now?" What do they say? What expressions do they have on their faces? Can this help you be compassionate and understanding in real life?

Now picture Jesus with you at your workplace, standing beside you. Jesus asks, "What can I do to help you here at work?" Tell him how he can help.

Now Jesus raises his hands in blessing and blesses you and your workplace.

QUESTIONS FOR JOURNALING

1. Take time for memory. Think of a time when things went really well at your workplace. Relive the sounds, sights, and feelings vividly, and then write about it.

2. What can you do to make your workspace a more compassionate, caring place?

3. How can your private prayer enhance your time at work?

chapter six

LOVING
Those in Need

In the 1960s, Belhaven was an all-white Presbyterian college in Jackson, Mississippi. I loved Belhaven. It was an excellent liberal arts school and a high percentage of students studied for Church vocations. The Scripture faculty modeled not only good scholarship but holiness as well. They loved us, and poured their hearts into our formation. Belhaven was a peaceful oasis for me amidst the turmoil of the sixties.

For Mississippi and much of the South, it was the era of violence against African Americans who were struggling to gain civil rights, and their supporters and allies. The Klan and its followers murdered Medgar Evers and many more civil rights workers, and burned forty African American churches. The Klan had also infiltrated the local and state police. They bombed the Jackson synagogue, trying to kill Rabbi Nussbaum, because of the hard work he and his congregation did in bringing about racial justice.

For my first year or so at Belhaven I put all this out of my mind and enjoyed the oasis of calm my school offered me. Then I had a dream that turned my life around. One Thanksgiving break, I had ridden the bus from Columbus, Georgia, back to Jackson. While the buses were supposedly integrated now, blacks still sat in the back of the bus, if they valued their safety. A middle-aged black woman sitting in the back of the bus was sobbing with near-uncontrollable grief. At a stop, the white driver stepped back into the bus, vigorously shook her, and condescendingly said, "Dry up, you are causing a scene."

I wondered if I should I go over and comfort her. After all, I was a candidate for the ministry and comforting the sorrowing is what ministers do. But fear struck my heart. What would the other passengers think of my going to the back of the bus? Would they think of me as a Freedom Rider and beat me to a pulp? Would the bus driver stop the bus and put me out? As much as I longed to go back to the woman and comfort her, I put my own safety above helping a fellow human.

Two days after returning to Belhaven, I dreamed of riding the bus again, only this time it was Jesus seated in the back of the bus sobbing. A loud thunderclap from a fall thunderstorm jarred me awake as I heard the words, "Find me on the back of the bus, or you won't find me at all." The dream jolted me into realizing something essential was missing from my spirituality: identifying and showing solidarity with those some might have considered the "least of these."

That dream led me to fervent prayer. As a result of that prayer, I realized I had to give and spend myself if I was to be a true servant. I involved myself in the civil rights movement in Jackson, meeting weekly with civil rights-oriented students of all races from the different campuses in that city. Belhaven finally accepted African American students my senior year. Since then the school has been a great example of progress in racial harmony and equality.

I learned especially from some of the African American

college students from Tougaloo University, a historically African American school in Jackson. One young woman, Rosa, shared with me the gift of her fierce anger over the poverty and brutality her family had experienced growing up in the cotton growing area of Mississippi called the Delta. Workers on the land were housed in dilapidated shacks, given little if any salary, and threatened with death if they left the landowner that "employed" them. Somehow she had made it through this and earned a scholarship to college.

One night when we were eating hamburgers and drinking Coke at a little restaurant adjacent to the Tougaloo campus called Mama T's, Rosa put it to me bluntly. "You have all your needs taken care of by your parents. You know nothing of what we go through. I bet you are proud you are so 'liberal,' and hanging out with people of color. You have to get down in the mess and get yourself messy if you really want to be part of our struggle." Her words cut me to the quick.

After that encounter with Rosa, I followed her advice as best I could. At one point I took part in an anti-Klan march after the bombing of the synagogue. So many risked much more than I did, accomplishing much more than I did, but at least I had begun on a small scale to realize what charity and service meant. Tougaloo was also bombed by the Klan. It tore me apart. In the weeks after the bombing I would often drive my car on the campus both day and late at night to make sure no Klansmen were there again to do harm, even though I knew there wasn't anything I could do if they came.

The next summer took me to another troubled part of the country: Lafayette Avenue Presbyterian Church, in the Fort

Greene section of Brooklyn. Though redeveloped today, then it was an extension of Bedford Stuyvesant: crime-ridden, filled with forgotten poor of our society. I led a street recreation program for children as part of my internship in becoming a Presbyterian minister. Because sports were difficult for me because of my disability, we hired several local teenagers to lead the sports and I supervised. We fed the children lunch and took them on outings to Manhattan to see beautiful things like the Cloisters and the Cathedral of St. John the Divine.

Pope Francis wrote in his 2013 Day for Life greeting that "even the weakest and most vulnerable, the sick, the old, the unborn and the poor, are masterpieces of God's creation, made in his own image, destined to live forever, and deserving of the utmost reverence and respect."[27] In Brooklyn I learned far more than I could ever teach. Despite the addiction, crime, and abuse found there, these children seemed close to God. They warmed to the simplest gestures of concern or caring. They brought me closer to God and made me aware of my own inner poverty. They changed my whole concept of what it means to be a Christian.

Often when people first experience God's love, they tend to view the spiritual life as a roadway to personal fulfillment and a happier family life. But true prayer eventually draws us beyond the purely personal. We begin to see that our individual healing is tied in with the healing of the whole world. Only as I open up myself to the cry of the poor, to their pain, can the healing process begin within me.

St. Paulinus of Nola speaks of the "association with the needy which heals our wounds."[28] The poor are our healing because their need for God, their need for grace, their need for love, is so apparent. How easily we mask our own poverty. Each of us is poor. Each of us is broken. Each of us needs God's love and grace. Each of us needs other people. We try desperately to hide these needs from ourselves and from others. Our wealth and material possessions can easily numb us to the very pain and the need that draw us close to God and one another. We place a high value on optimism, competition, and being on top of things. The apostle Paul calls us to weep with those who weep and rejoice with those who rejoice. Unless we are willing to feel the depths of pain, our ability to feel joy and laughter leaves us also. Part of our hesitation is that we see ourselves as breakable. By taking in some of the pain of the world, we fear we would be shattered.

The disabled, the outcasts, the emotionally wounded, those denied justice, who live in a state of emotional and physical starvation, can't hide their need. If we dare make ourselves vulnerable to them, we experience the depth of our own poverty. Vulnerability to the poor brings a wondrous grace to us. When our sister's pain and our brother's pain becomes our pain, we are drawn beyond ourselves. Relationships with the hurting and ostracized are critical if our relationships are to be whole and full. We need to cultivate compassion when we pray. Emptying ourselves for the sake of others in service is at the heart of spirituality.

Pope Francis has said "This is why I want a Church which is poor and for the poor. They have much to teach us. Not only do they share in the *sensus fidei* (sense of the faith), but in their difficulties they know the suffering Christ. We need to let ourselves be evangelized by them."[29]

Redemption involves the whole created universe. We are not saved alone; we are not healed alone. We are healed together in community with other human beings. We are saved and healed together, in relationship, with the whole universe. Paul says, "With all wisdom and insight he has made known to us the mystery of his will, according to his good pleasure that he set forth in Christ, as a plan for the fullness of time, to gather up all things in him, things in heaven and things on earth" (Ephesians 1:8–10). And again, "He has put all things under his feet and has made him the head over all things for the church, which is his body, the fullness of him who fills all in all" (Ephesians 1:22–23). I cannot be healed unless I am open to all creation being healed. That opening opens me to Christ's healing.

We are called to let Jesus wash our feet and then go out and wash the feet of others. Scripture scholar Raymond Brown describes the service to which all believers are called and of which deacons are a sign:

> In demeaning himself to wash his disciples' feet Jesus is acting out beforehand his humiliation and death...the foot washing is an action of service to others, symbolic of the service he will render in laying down his life for others; that is why Jesus can claim that the foot washing is necessary if the disciples are to share in his heritage and that it will render the disciples clean.[30]

Relationship with the disadvantaged also means doing the very mundane service of feeding the hungry, giving dignity to those thrown away. Perhaps it could mean volunteering at a soup kitchen or your parish or diocesan ministry to the poor. A friend in Austin has developed a unique way to help the poor. He makes up packets of nutritious food to give to anyone he meets who is asking for a handout.

Relationship with the poor also means taking on the structural causes of poverty. The National Center for Children in Poverty sums it up: "Poverty is the single greatest threat to children's well-being. But effective public policies—to make work pay for low-income parents and to provide high-quality early care and learning experiences for their children—can make a difference. Investments in the most vulnerable children are also critical."[31]

In his first trip outside the Vatican, Pope Francis traveled to Lampedusa island, part of Italy not far from the African coast, where thousands of refugees from Africa suffer. Many have been lost at sea on their way there. In his homily, Pope Francis spoke of the "globalization of indifference." He said the suffering of others no longer bothers us in the culture we live in. He continued, "We are a society that has forgotten the experience of weeping, of 'suffering with'... The globalization of indifference has taken from us the ability to weep!"

Pope Francis prayed, "We ask for forgiveness for the indifference toward so many brothers and sisters, we ask forgiveness for those who are pleased with themselves, who are closed in on their own well-being in a way that leads to the anesthesia of the heart."[32]

Part of spirituality is letting God give us tender hearts that weep and suffer with our hurting brothers and sisters. The meditation in this chapter is intended for developing compassion for all who suffer, for our suffering world.

On her website Spiritual Practices for Activists, Joanna Macy says, "In that context, the pain we feel for our world is a living testimony to our interconnectedness with it. If we deny this pain, we become like blocked and atrophied neurons, deprived of life's flow and weakening the larger body in which we take being. But if we let it move through us, we affirm our belonging; our collective awareness increases. We can open to the pain of the world in confidence that it can neither shatter nor isolate us, for we are not objects that can break. We are resilient patterns within a vaster web of knowing."[33]

When we open ourselves to the pain of the world, we experience resilience—a resilience that comes from Christ's love that upholds and unifies all that is. The following meditation can help you allow painful information to pass through you without shattering you. A wise person once said, "Let all sorrows ripen in me." Prayer can help us make rich compost out of the grief of the world. Meditative prayer can expand the breadth of our compassion. We accept the pain of the world and allow it to pass through us.

TIME FOR HEALING PRAYER
A Prayer

Dear Jesus, help us to encounter your presence in those whom society neglects or rejects. You have said the measure of how close we are to you is the measure of how close we are to them. May they not repel us, but become a source of joy, for when we love them, we love you. Sensitize our hearts to the needs of all your children, and guide our hands in helping them. May we see your face in everyone we encounter, especially the most helpless. Amen.

SCRIPTURE TO PONDER

Is not this the fast that I choose:
  to loose the bonds of injustice,
  to undo the thongs of the yoke,

to let the oppressed go free,
  and to break every yoke?

Is it not to share your bread with the hungry,
  and bring the homeless poor into your house;
when you see the naked, to cover them,
  and not to hide yourself from your own kin?

Then your light shall break forth like the dawn,
  and your healing shall spring up quickly;
your vindicator shall go before you,
  the glory of the Lord shall be your rearguard.
Then you shall call, and the Lord will answer;
you shall cry for help, and he will say, Here I am.

If you remove the yoke from among you,
  the pointing of the finger, the speaking of evil,
if you offer your food to the hungry
  and satisfy the needs of the afflicted,
then your light shall rise in the darkness
  and your gloom be like the noonday.
The Lord will guide you continually,
  and satisfy your needs in parched places,
  and make your bones strong;
and you shall be like a watered garden,
  like a spring of water,
  whose waters never fail.
Your ancient ruins shall be rebuilt;
  you shall raise up the foundations of many generations;
you shall be called the repairer of the breach,
  the restorer of streets to live in. (Isaiah 58:6–12)

GUIDED MEDITATION

Relax. Be still. Imagine that you are surrounded by the light of God's presence. In the midst of that light stands Jesus. His healing light penetrates you with the warmth, the glow of his love. An egg-shaped sphere of the light of his love surrounds you. Have a sense of that love encompassing you.

Jesus takes your hand in his. You feel the warmth of his love flow from his hand to yours through your arms into your entire body and soul. With your hand you feel the wounds on the hand that clasps yours. You know that this is how much he loves you. As you hold his hands you feel a wound in your hands like his, a wound in your side too. The wounds in you, like his are for the rejected, the outcasts, the untouchables, victims of injustice.

Now Jesus says, "I want to show you some scenes. See with your heart. Listen with your heart."

Now allow images of your fellow human beings to emerge—images of people who are hurting, needy, alienated, sick, imprisoned, or on battlefields. There is no need to strain for these images. They are already there, waiting to come forward, by virtue of the fact that we are knitted with creation. Let them gather inside you like a dark liquid. Be open to the pain of the universe, the animals, trees, seas, air.

Notice your breathing, your breathing in and your breathing out. Each time you inhale, you breathe in God's love; each time you exhale you breathe out pain. Feel the pain leave you, absorbed by the light of God's love that surrounds. Breathe out your pain, the world's pain that you have taken on. Feel the light of God's love.

QUESTIONS FOR JOURNALING

1. Write about a time you were in need, physically, emotionally, or spirituality, and others reached out to help. What was that like for you?

2. What can you do to help those in need?

3. What can you do to help change unjust structures to merciful structures?

~chapter seven~

LOVING
Our Neighbor
Requires Communication

Listening is the key to good communication. On the surface, it seems like technology has made communication much easier. At the touch of a button we can exchange words, even pictures, with one another. Though it may seem that we are communicating more, we often are communicating less. Texting or e-mailing removes much of the human element—tone of voice, body language—and we miss out on interpersonal cues that inflection or facial expressions give us.

Families, it seems, are busier than ever these days. Many don't have time for a shared family meal to sum up their days and celebrate joys, successes, share troubles and concerns. A son might have football practice, a daughter might have a part-time job, and Mom is busy taking an after-hours work-related call. The interruption of texts, e-mails, and Tweets intrudes more and more into conversations. We have more means of communication, but communicate less.

Rather than texting or e-mailing, try picking up the phone and calling for more intimate or personal issues. Better yet, meet face-to-face; it's kinder and breeds closeness. Personal communication encourages us take responsibility for our own thoughts and feelings.

An engaged couple, Pat and Rodney, nearly lost their relationship because they were communicating primarily through texting. Rodney had great difficulty communicating on a personal level. He held tightly to his emotions. While he enjoyed the closeness of the couple's embraces and enjoyed bowling and movies with Pat, he couldn't articulate his emotional needs. Instead, he texted to get to the core of whatever bothered him. In one text he wrote, "You talk too much, and it's all about yourself. And you embarrass me by the ill matching clothes you sometimes wear. Is that how little you care about me?"

She texted back, "Are you trying to control me?"

They had supper together the next evening and Pat asked, "Can we talk about the fight we just had?"

"What fight?" Rodney asked, raising his voice.

"In our texts," Pat told him, her voice breaking.

"It was just texting. You are sensitive, too sensitive."

In tears, Pat fled to the ladies' room. It took ten minutes for her to come out. The ride home in Rodney's car was filled with cold silence.

When Pat got up the next morning she found the text, "Who do you think you are embarrassing me like that where the whole restaurant could see?"

She followed up with this text, "Go to hell."

When they were together in person, neither talked about the texts. Their relationship grew very cold. After several weeks, Rodney got this text during his lunch break at work: "Don't you think we should consider calling off this wedding?"

Startled by this message, Rodney called Pat and finally talked personally to her with a tinge of desperation in his voice, "I love you. I love you and I don't want to lose you. I'll do anything."

"Will you come to couple's counseling with me?"

Rodney hesitated, but then said yes. They started going to couple's therapy at the nearby pastoral center. They did not cancel their engagement, but did postpone their wedding a while.

In counseling, they learned loving ways to communicate in person. Even more important, their counselor taught them how to pray as a couple. Every night before they parted they held hands and prayed together. More than anything else this drew them close. The counselor asked them to imagine Jesus seated near them and to talk to him as they would a friend.

The two drew closer together than they dreamed possible and when their wedding date came around, they were both ready.

In our close relationships, listening is far more important than talking. Listening requires empathy, feeling and sensing some of what the other person senses and feels. Show you are listening by making eye contact and asking follow-up questions. Once you think you are truly hearing what the other person says on an emotional level, reflect it back to them.

Bringing up issues is a vital part of any relationship. But instead of using "you" language use "I" language. When you do that, you are not blaming or causing guilt. For instance, if a husband comes home and says to his wife, "You never have time for me anymore," that's harsh and blaming language. When we do that we take the high place of judgment and look down on the other. Instead, he might say, "I feel as if ever since you took on that afternoon job and became involved in our parish's social ministry, you haven't had time for me anymore. I feel deserted, as though I am no longer at the top of your priorities list. I wish things were like they used to be." A phrase like this puts you on an even playing field and makes room for healing, while not pushing the issue under the rug.

This approach does not dodge or minimize the issue, but offers the possibility of truly understanding each other. If you are in a relationship that is weighed down by the way you communicate, the sad news is if you keep doing it the same way, your relationship can become further mired. The happy news is if you really try to listen, use "I" language, and good communication skills, things can get a lot better fairly soon.

Jonathan Robinson, in his book *Communication Miracles for Couples,* offers advice on communication that applies not only to couples, but to close friends and relatives as well. One of these is what he calls "acknowledgment." Acknowledgment means agreeing that what your partner, friend, or relative says they feel is what they feel. You don't have to agree that they are right or that it is necessarily so, but that it is their perspective. For instance, a further answer to the partner who said, "You never have time for me anymore" is to say, "You are hurting and feeling isolated right now. You are hungry for the intimacy we once had." By empathizing you let them know you understand their perspective. You will be amazed at how quickly they will open up to your feelings and perspective in return. In addition, it helps if you can make a deposit in what Robinson calls their "self-esteem bank." In this case, you might say, "I know you are saying this because you love me and want to be close. I want that too."

This validating of the other's experience builds trust, and trust is essential for close relationships. Seek first to understand and then to be understood. Robinson has developed what he calls his "acknowledgment formula":

> In a sentence, sum up how your friend or partner is experiencing things.

> Tune in to what they must be feeling and reflect it back. "You must feel" is a good phrase to start out with.

> If negative emotions are acknowledged say, "I'm sorry you feel that way. I'm sad you feel that hurt."

All this doesn't mean you can't get into solutions with the person, but people usually need lots of understanding and acknowledgment before they can be open to solutions. As Robinson puts it, "The more lovingly you offer your acknowledgement the sooner (that person) will be open to other things you have to say."[34]

A second way to build a great climate for communication in friendships or marriages is to practice what Robinson calls "appreciation." This is different from acknowledgement. You use your mind to think of the things about your friend or spouse that you like, listen to your emotions to find positive feelings you have toward the other, then express that appreciation. For this to work you should do it often. Above all else you should be truthful. Rather than a general phrase such as "you are always nice," be specific. Say something like this: "I liked it when you helped that elderly and isolated woman in your neighborhood by cutting her grass and then visiting with her. You do so many kind and caring things for me, too, like washing my car, and remembering my birthday by inviting me for a special lunch."

For so many of us opening up to someone we care about can make us feel anxious. Perhaps in the past, especially in our childhood, we revealed ourselves to others and were slammed down, perhaps made to feel small. These past put-downs leave scars. When we try to trust in the present moment, the past rushes in to kidnap the present. We not only remember when we were hurt, we experience again the feelings of rejection.

The 1946 film *Deception* tells the story of Christine. Played by Bette Davis, she is the lover of a wealthy man whose money helps her live lavishly. She then ends the romantic part of relationship in order to marry a man she truly loves. She does not tell her new husband about her involvement with her former wealthy lover. Yet he suspects she is involved with someone else, especially when he meets the wealthy man whom she introduces as "just a friend." The husband thinks he cannot really trust what she says to him.

Meanwhile the wealthy man threatens to reveal their relationship. The Bette Davis character kills him rather than let him expose her. In the final scene of the movie she has a bombshell disclosure to her husband. She confesses and tells him the whole story. In finally telling the truth, she became worthy of trust. Once she shared her secret, her face showed relief and an uncharacteristic calm.

When she held off telling her husband, she was showing she didn't trust him, in essence saying, "If I unveil myself to you, you may cause trouble and harm me. You may well abandon me."

Only when it was too late did she trust. So many friendships and marriages fail because they do not build trust soon enough. Trust says, "I can be close to you; I can be intimate with you; when needed I can tell you my secrets."

By using a journal or seeing a therapist, we can let go of the negative feelings the memory holds. We will always remember it as a fact in our past, but the old emotions will not sabotage closeness in the present.

Even more than counseling or journaling, prayer can help us deal with past trauma. We can converse with God as a friend and tell him our secrets. If it is big enough to cause me anxiety it's big enough for me to talk out with God. One especially good way of dealing with these past traumas is through imaginative prayer. In imaginative meditation you relive the scenes of hurt. But in this case, you imagine that Jesus is there with you. He takes your hand and prevents harm from coming to you.

I think of a young couple, Jill and Arthur, when I think of imaginative prayer. Arthur had grown up in a home with an alcoholic and abusive father. When sober, which was about eighty percent of the time, Arthur's father was a caring and wise husband and father. When he was intoxicated, he verbally and sometimes physically abused Arthur. In one traumatic event, his father confronted him when he found out that his son had struck out at the afternoon baseball game. He yelled at him, "You are a failure and no son of mine is going to be a failure. I'm ashamed you were ever born." Then he rammed his fist into the plaster wall. Arthur's growing up years were filled with similar scenes.

The result was that Arthur had great difficulty in trusting Jill's love or anyone else's love for that matter. Much of his capacity to even feel had been shut down by the scenes of hurt. Jill knew that something was amiss. She had come from a normal, loving home, and felt rejected when Arthur failed to tell her his emotions or to reflect back to her feelings when she shared some intimate words with him.

Jill finally confronted him with this, but in a loving way. "You help out so much with housework and cooking. You are strong when I need you to be strong, but somehow I feel as if we are not close. Even when you are there, you are not there. Something major is missing in our relationship. I love you, but I am hurting terribly. I feel so lonely, even in your presence." She then suggested they see a deacon who was a trained pastoral counselor to help them with their relationship.

Reluctantly, Arthur agreed. In the first session the deacon asked each of them to tell him something of their family of origin. Jill talked about the fun she had with her sisters and parents and what a blow the death of grandmother was when she was fifteen. When his turn came, Arthur started out by telling how good he was at baseball growing up, but froze a few seconds afterward, holding his breath. Fear crossed his face like a tornado over the plain. He fidgeted in such a way that it looked like he wanted to get up and run.

"What's wrong?" the deacon asked. "You seem frightened."

Then choking on his words, Arthur said, "I do feel afraid, so very afraid, but I don't know why." Jill took his hand and that calmed him a bit.

"Jill, I love you, but I'm not ready to talk about my past with you."

The deacon then suggested that Arthur come in by himself for counseling the next week. Couple's counseling could wait. In that follow-up session the deacon started off talking baseball and sports with Arthur until he felt more comfortable. Then the deacon asked, "I noticed you had a hard time talking about your past last week. I want you to feel so very safe. Everything you say here is confidential; it's between you, me, and God."

"Jill can't know, she just can't know."

"I won't tell her, this is just you and me."

Arthur blurted out, "I grew up with an alcoholic father. I'm afraid Jill won't love me if she knows."

"That your Dad was an alcoholic?"

"No, the details," Arthur replied.

"It's scary for you, isn't it?"

"Yes, I feel like I will come totally unglued if I tell. I'll go crazy."

Both the deacon and Arthur agreed that individual counseling, just with Arthur, should continue for a few weeks. Slowly, Arthur began to unburden his heart to the deacon. They closed each session with prayer and a meditation led by the deacon. He slowly introduced Arthur to a way of meditation to drain out the sting of hurtful memories.

In the meditations, he had Arthur vividly imagine the scenes of pain and then picture Jesus in those scenes healing the feelings of hurt and fear. For instance, when the deacon had him reimagine the scene where his father berated him, Jesus was there holding his hand. After his father said, "I am ashamed you were even born," Jesus, holding Arthur's hand, says, "This isn't so. You are my dear and precious child. Rest in my love."

After a few weeks of counseling and meditation, Arthur could begin to tell about his childhood hurts, but this time as a fact of his past without the dread, shame, and fear. Finally, after about eight weeks of counseling and prayer, Arthur said to the deacon, "I want to tell Jill now. It's time."

"Do you want me to bring Jill back into counseling, so the three of us can talk it over?"

"Not now, I want to tell her alone."

That evening he did tell her, racked with sobs. Jill moved them to the large couch where she held him tightly and warmly as the sobs convulsed through him.

After they held each other a while, she said, "I feel so close to you, now, closer than I have ever felt."

That evening marked a bright new day in their marriage. They began to share feelings and intimate conversation with each other. They went to couple's counseling a few more times with the deacon to fine tune their new relationship. Arthur and Jill rejoiced that trust had been restored and a whole new level of communication begun.

I've noticed how coming to grips with the past has built trust in my own relationships. I've previously mentioned that I grew up in a dysfunctional home. This led to my own difficulty in trusting human relationships. It was hard for me to believe my friends actually loved me. In my early adulthood I could become clinging and possessive of my friends. Thankfully my friends were mature enough that they kept up the friendships.

For me, trusting others first meant trusting in God. In my early twenties, after devouring Thomas Merton's writings and reading the *Philokalia*, a compendium of writings from the Eastern Fathers on spirituality, I began a contemplative prayer life, taking time to bask in the love of God and rest in his present. The deep silences of God refreshed my heart and filled me with love deep inside. Wrapped in the safety of his presence, feelings of shame began to slip away.

It made it easier to share my history with others. Paul Evans, my spiritual friend from Belhaven College, was the first person I told about the painful times in my life. I told him in an almost clinical manner, not letting the emotions of that time come out. It was just too painful. Opening up about the shame and terror I felt was a slow process. The more I conveyed those feelings, however, the easier it was to trust others.

When I first opened up about my traumatic brain injury and the difficulties that had come from it, I could talk about how some of my peers and teachers would shame me because of my disability, but not my parents' role. I loved my parents dearly and most of the time they were good and loving parents. Then I realized that if I also talked about them in context, speaking about wonderful things they had done for me like paying for my higher education and the kindness they showed me later in my adulthood, I should feel free to talk.

I first opened up about my cognitive disability when I wrote *Visions: The Soul's Path to the Sacred*. I told the basics, but not my parents' role. Outside of close friends like Deacon Robert Herrmann and Paul Evans, I had talked little of my disability. It was profoundly healing to trust that knowledge to my readers. Then, in a sermon, I trusted my congregation by talking about my disability. All this allowed me to draw closer to people, especially my parish family, who met the news with abundant love and greater closeness. After that, it was far easier for me to talk freely about any subject, not just my disability.

Now to be real and effective in my ministry I need to write about how the problems in my home affected me. Each time I share a different level of my heart, a deeper level of trust develops between me, my close friends, and my cousins, the only family I have left. Fully coming to grips with the past and fully trusting takes a lifetime.

TIME FOR HEALING PRAYER
A Prayer

Dear Lord, you are the master of good communication. You communicated your love and commandments in the Hebrew Scriptures. You communicated ultimately through your Son. You converse with us through the Scriptures and through the physical touches that are your sacraments. You speak peace to our hearts through the stillness of prayer. You reveal your splendor to us in the beauty of creation. Please help us communicate with each other. Help us all to see others as precious children of yours who are to be respected, treated with dignity, and loved. Help us affirm and not blame or accuse. Help us to converse with each other with truth as well as love. Turn our hearts from conflict to caring. Teach us to trust. Amen.

SCRIPTURE TO PONDER

So we, who are many, are one body in Christ, and individually we are members one of another. We have gifts that differ according to the grace given to us: prophecy, in proportion to faith; ministry, in ministering; the teacher, in teaching; the exhorter, in exhortation; the giver, in generosity; the leader, in diligence; the compassionate, in cheerfulness. Let love be genuine; hate what is evil, hold fast to what is good; love one another with mutual affection; outdo one another in showing honor. Do not lag in zeal, be ardent in spirit, serve the Lord. Rejoice in hope, be patient in suffering, persevere in prayer. Contribute to the needs of the saints; extend hospitality to strangers. Bless those who persecute you; bless and do not curse them. Rejoice with those who rejoice, weep with those who weep. (Romans 12:5–15)

GUIDED MEDITATION

Quiet down and notice your breathing in and out. Perhaps repeat the name of Jesus over and over. Think back and as vividly as possible remember a time when God communicated his love to you. Visualize a scene when another person communicated with you, acknowledging you, appreciating you.

Remember some times when you communicated with others well. What made that communication so effective?

Now let the eye of your heart turn to someone you care about but with whom communication is difficult. Picture that person sitting in front of you, facing you. Jesus stands by you, reassuring you with his hand on your shoulder. Your soul stirs because Jesus is so near. Your confidence is buoyed because of his presence.

First think of some of the difficulties that the person facing you has expressed to you. With Jesus's help, acknowledge what they feel through your words. How does the other person react?

Now look at that person's face. Get in touch with the things you appreciate in that person. Tell them what you appreciate. How do they react?

Jesus invites the other person to get out of the chair and join the two of you. Jesus embraces the two of you as the timeless peace of God pours over the three of you.

QUESTIONS FOR JOURNALING

1. Write about a time you truly trusted someone and your trust was rewarded with greater closeness.
2. Write about a time when someone trusted you.
3. How can prayer, communication with God, help your communication with other people?

chapter eight

LOVING
Our Neighbor
Requires Dealing with
Conflict

In this chapter, we continue on the theme of communication, zeroing in on the role of conflict in a relationship. In any close friendship, marriage, family, or work relationship, conflict is inevitable. Insisting on being right and blaming can cause a kaleidoscope of hurt and pain and pull the relationship further apart. What is important is that we allow the conflict to draw us nearer and build an even stronger relationship.

Whenever you have a conflict or a heated topic to talk over with a coworker, friend, or spouse, talk it over with God before you talk to that person about it. You will then find it much easier to talk to the other person. Taking time for meditation before confronting the other person is of utmost importance.

In conflict resolution, it is equally important to know what you want as well as how you feel. For instance, how would you like the other person to behave? Put in one sentence the behavior you want to see in the other. Then meditate on it. When has there been a time when you experienced this good behavior and how did it affect you? Think of when the other person experienced that kind of behavior and felt it benefitted them.

Try to put the feeling into a word picture, or metaphor, which captures its essence. Start off with the words, "I feel as if…" Word pictures go straight to the heart and can become channels of great communication.

Anne, a nurse, and Lois, a police officer, were friends since their young adulthood. They often had lunch together, babysat each other's children, and now they both served on the parish council together. They had been confidants who had many good times together. They occasionally fought, but always stayed together as friends. Now they found themselves poles apart on several issues facing the council. Those disagreements seeped into their personal relationship, uncovering fissures that had long lain dormant.

The first major issue was whether to close the parish's school or not. Those who wanted to close it said that because of diminishing enrollment, the school had become a huge burden to the parish, costing about $100,000 in subsidy and taking away vital funds needed to sustain other ministries. Anne wanted to keep it open while Lois wanted to close it and use the funds partly to develop a top-notch religious education ministry. In one council meeting, Lois flew into a tirade at Anne, saying, "You are just trying to control this situation when it's uncontrollable, just like you are always trying to control me. You're the one to pick the restaurant when we go out to lunch. You run from unpleasant choices. And I know your husband and kids feel that control, too. I can see it on their faces. You have always sugarcoated reality and tried to control it in order to keep everything looking rosy. I, for one, am tired of your control."

Anne ran from the room in tears. In her despair over the state of their relationship, she remembered a talk she had heard on prayer and meditation in relationships and took time to pray about her relationship with Lois. She also pulled out her spiritual journal, a tool she had learned to use on a retreat many years before.

First, she wanted to get in touch with what she had been feeling and poured out her emotions in her journal. She wrote about the jumble of emotions she felt after Lois's tirade. She wrote about her anger, fear, and hurt, feeling down, and somehow guilty at the same time. After journaling about her feelings she wrote out a prayer:

> Dear Lord, Lois has been a wonderful part of my life for over twenty years. We have shared many fine, even beautiful, times together. Now our friendship is in shambles. I'm sad, but also fiercely angry. How dare Lois speak to me like that? I'm hurting. It's almost like hearing a loved one has died. I thought our friendship was sacred. Please help bring healing to this relationship. Help us to love each other again and guide my words that they might be healing. Amen.

Next Anne wrote down the emotion she felt most: "Loss." Then she asked herself about a similar time Lois felt loss with some of the same desperation. She remembered how hard it was for Lois to lose her teenage brother who was killed while crossing a busy street. She then wrote out some word pictures that expressed the feelings involved. Anne then wrote down the particular behavior she wanted Lois to change. She wanted Lois to stop accusing and return to the supportive words that had been characteristic of most of their relationship.

Anne finally took the step of calling Lois. She asked, "Would it be possible, would you have time, for us to talk?"

Lois, to Anne's relief, agreed and invited Anne over for coffee. After a bit of awkward silence as they sat there drinking coffee, Anne began by acknowledging Lois's emotions. "I know you care passionately about closing the school. That's one of the things I have always liked about you, your intense caring and concern. However I feel like the dispute over the school has turned our friendship into a battleground," Anne continued.

"Somehow, things between us are not what they used to be. I feel almost like I have lost a loved one, feeling like you felt when your little brother was killed. Ours has been a life-giving friendship for so long and your supportive words and actions have been so much a part of it. Now your words seem accusatory. I want our friendship to go back to being caring and supporting as it has been through the years. I'd like to hear you speak to me with the same warmth you used to speak to me. I know we disagree over the school, but that's not the kind of disagreement that should poison our friendship.

"I remember how energizing it was for you when our pastor affirmed you for the Christmas play. That's the feeling I want us to have when I am together with you. I feel like our friendship has been a battleground, and I want it again, instead, to be like a peaceful meadow.

"I know, like you say, there are times I have been too controlling. Thanks for pointing this out to me. I'm so sorry for the pain this must give you. With your help, I want to do better, much better. I really long to hear kind words from you."

At this, tears began to course down Lois's face. "I too, have missed the way our friendship used to be. I treasure many of the times we have been together. I do need to watch my tongue and better express my emotions."

That conversation marked the beginning of a healing of their friendship. Anne's words were "miracle words," made possible because she took time to pray and meditate on which words she would use.

Different opinions about the school closing or staying open ceased to be a roadblock to their friendship. They both realized that friends can have different opinions. In the end, the decision was taken out of the parish council's hands when the diocese closed the school for having not enough students and instead invited the students to attend a thriving school in a nearby parish.

We all get angry from time to time. Anger is a natural human emotion. God put it in us for a reason. Anger is like fire. Fire can light a votive candle; in a fireplace it can warm a room. A lit candle can be a sign of the Resurrection. It can accomplish these things with great care. Anger protects us from becoming a doormat. It can aid us in protecting the innocent and vulnerable.

Yet fire, if not handled carefully, can burn down half of Southern California. So it is with anger. Out of control it can wreak emotional havoc in relationships. Emotional outbursts that interfere with conversations meant to heal conflict can debilitate us and ruin cooperation. They can make it difficult to speak to and treat others with dignity and respect. Cato wrote, "An angry man opens his mouth and shuts his eyes."[35] Stories of road rage, shootings, domestic violence, riots, and terrorist attacks fill the news. Much toxic political discourse and some popular music are just rants. Everywhere around us we see examples of rage out of control. It can be easy for us to act out in similar ways.

Carol Tavris in her book, *Anger: The Misunderstood Emotion*, writes, "I have watched people use anger in the name of emotional liberation, whittle away their spirits in bitterness and revenge... And I watch with admiration those who use anger to probe for the truth... who challenge and change the complacent injustices of life."[36]

As Les and Leslie Parrott put it in their book on conflict in couples, *The Good Fight*, "It's often destructive, it's often a waste, but every once in a while it works. It can fuel our drive to achieve, help us maintain our self-respect, or stop the world from walking all over us."[37]

Handling and channeling anger well requires prayer and meditation. The psalmist often pours out his anger in the presence of God. What better place is there to leave our anger than at the feet of God? We can journal about our anger, pour it out on paper, concretize it. The act of writing helps us objectify the anger and get it down to size. In doing so, we can pray about constructive ways to use it.

Renaissance writer Michel de Montaigne urged people to channel anger with care to "husband their anger and not expend it at random, for that impedes its effect and weight. Heedless and continual scolding becomes a habit and makes everyone discount it."[38]

There is a point when anger gets too revved up and turns into a major forest fire, destructive and all consuming. Proverbs 29:11 says: "Fools give full vent to their rage, but the wise bring calm in the end" (*NIV*). This bringing "calm in the end" is fruit of prayerfully channeling anger.

Some friends and relatives seem especially prone to anger. Often this finds its origin in early mistreatment, or a lack of healthy models of relationships while growing up. In addition, some people seem more biologically prone to anger.

The Parrotts suggest some ways of taming the temper. One is to "do nothing." When your heart beats rapidly with anger and your blood heats up, perhaps the first thing is to keep silent until you have had a chance to pray and meditate. Waiting awhile is not the same as denying and stuffing in our anger. Thomas Jefferson recommended counting to ten or, if the anger was particularly strong, counting to a hundred. The very act of counting is a distraction that keeps us, for a while, from adding more fuel to the fire. Deep breathing, or noticing your breathing, can also help us get past that initial burst of rage.

Sometimes a person we love can have a major problem such as addiction, a mental illness that needs intervention. Major conflict can come from this. When we deal with a close other who has such a problem, our response is most human: intense anger. Sometimes even with others present an intervention wouldn't work. I remember a spiritual friend of mine, William, whom I had known for a number of years. He was a highly successful attorney who was a member of my parish, a devout Christian, and one of the kindest and most giving people I have ever known. Whenever I, or others, appreciated his goodness or affirmed his success he would recite a poem about a man who seemed so well to everyone else yet went out and killed himself. More and more he looked listless, bottled up, and depressed.

Some other friends and I decided we had to do something. Our friend needed help, whatever his seeming success. We prayed and meditated on this for some time, thinking through his situation. Finally, we invited him over to the house for supper and talked earnestly. We reminded him of the funereal poem he often recited and assured him of our love and support. We prayed together with him and afterward he agreed to seek professional therapy and to attend emotional healing retreats. In a few months' time we noticed a new vigor in his step and new brightness in his eyes. He had begun dealing with abuse from childhood by an alcoholic father. Intervention, after prayer and meditation, worked in his case.

Sometimes loving confrontation does not work so readily. In those cases we need to pray and meditate and turn to God for wisdom to handle things wisely when the time comes. We cannot change the other with a magic word, but we can bear our inmost parts to the one love that turns the cosmos. We can allow God to change us so we will be able to say and do the right thing when the moment presents itself.

John, a family physician, faced such a difficult problem: His wife, June, suffered from alcoholism—yet she refused to recognize her disease. At times she would lash out at their two daughters, aged nine and ten, calling them lazy, worthless, and not fit to be her daughters. Then an hour or two after her tirades, she turned into the picture of a loving mother, doting on her children. Her moods swung swiftly. At times when she was supposed to be watching the girls, she lay sprawled out on her bed instead. Once when she lay passed out on the bed, the younger daughter started a kitchen fire while attempting to cook lunch. John himself experienced both her hostility and her loving side. Her changes in mood left him constantly drained and on guard. John felt abandoned and alone in dealing with his wife's problems. He seemed to have no one to whom he could turn.

He had always thought of their first twelve years of marriage as wonderful. Before the alcohol took over, he thought June was the best wife anyone could hope for. They had lived their lives in close harmony. But now, worry about his wife and the future of his family gripped him both day and night. Scenarios of dire outcomes passed before him. Would his wife's neglect of the children result in their injury? After all, the kitchen fire was a close call. He worried that his wife's verbal abuse of the two girls would permanently scar them. These worries caused sleepless nights and wore him out to the point that he seemed lethargic. He also had to cope with a growing anger at his wife for her behavior.

Drained of energy by his worries and anger, he found it difficult to be fully alert while seeing patients. He worried about accidentally making medical mistakes in his practice because of his condition. His options seemed few. Divorcing his wife would be near impossible for him; he believed in the permanence of marriage. Moreover, he could not be certain he would be awarded custody of the children. Any time he mentioned treatment, no matter how loving his manner, June raged and denied that she even had an alcohol problem. John's worries left him so beaten down that he found it nearly impossible to take any action at all to resolve the family's problems. No matter how hard he pleaded, June would not even consider treatment.

In desperation, John approached one of his parish's deacons for help. The deacon, a caring listener, just encouraged John to unload his worries. After John finished, the deacon said in a soft tone, "You need to begin taking care of yourself. Cut your hours at work. Take time for long walks, for going fishing with your buddies. Most of all pray, read Scripture, come to daily Mass when possible, and meditate to pry open the doors of wisdom in your heart." Then the deacon prayed with him, gave him a blessing, and closed by reading the following Scripture, "Peace I leave with you; my peace I give to you. I do not give to you as the world gives. Do not let your hearts be troubled, and do not let them be afraid" (John 14:27).

John memorized that Bible verse and repeated it slowly and silently throughout his day. He arrived at his office early to pray and read Scripture. Daily he unburdened himself to God in his prayer, pouring out his worries and anger. He made a special point of praying for his wife and her recovery every day. As he did this, his anger at his wife dissipated. It was replaced by compassion and tenderness. He realized that his wife's addiction to alcohol must be terrible for her. He imagined her loneliness, her fear of being held in the grip of a disease she could not control. His worries lost some of their crippling force.

Then everything turned worse. In deep winter, June and their ten-year-old daughter drove around town, running errands. Not in control of herself, June left her daughter in the car as she went into a bar. "One small drink would not hurt," June thought. "I'll be finished in there in just a minute." One drink turned into three. The minute turned into an hour. When June returned to her car, she found her daughter shaking all over because of the cold. She saw the beginnings of frostbite on her daughter's face. Panicked, she called John, honestly told him what happened and asked him to rush over. She embraced her daughter, saying repeatedly, "I'm so sorry, sweetheart, at what I've done to you."

When John arrived, he moved his frightened daughter to his car and quickly drove to the emergency room. After examining her, the doctor assured John that there would be no permanent physical scarring, and sent the father and daughter home with prescriptions of different lotions to use on her face. They found June at home, curled on the bed in a fetal position, with her fists tightened up.

Before he began seeing the deacon and praying daily for his wife, John's anger might have overpowered him, causing him to severely chastise his wife. Now his heart opened wide with compassion and devotion to her. He walked over to the bed, lay down beside his wife, tenderly embracing her, and in a voice choked with tears said, "I love you, June, more than I can ever express. I will always love you, be sure of that. Until the disease took over, you were the brightness in my life, and you will be again. It's time, June, its time to get treatment."

She whispered back to him, "I know, dear. It's time." The next morning she entered rehabilitation and has now been sober for two years. Like all alcoholics, she will always be in recovery, but now she has help.

Time for Healing Prayer
A Prayer

Dear Lord, you reconciled us to yourself and all creation. Through your love which is so deep, you took creation's pain upon yourself: our pain, our family's pain, the pain in so many of our relationships. Your love is the medicine for any brokenness in our relationships. Enable us to love our neighbor with the calm and purity with which you love us. Give us the words to work through conflict and agitation to true peace. Just as you have given us peace, help us spread this peace to others in thought, word, and deed. When hurt interferes with us loving our neighbor, remind us to turn to you for wisdom and calm. Amen.

For if we are beside ourselves, it is for God; if we are in our right mind, it is for you. For the love of Christ urges us on, because we are convinced that one has died for all; therefore all have died. And he died for all, so that those who live might live no longer for themselves, but for him who died and was raised for them.

From now on, therefore, we regard no one from a human point of view; even though we once knew Christ from a human point of view, we know him no longer in that way. So if anyone is in Christ, there is a new creation: everything old has passed away; see, everything has become new! All this is from God, who reconciled us to himself through Christ, and has given us the ministry of reconciliation; that is, in Christ, God was reconciling the world to himself, not counting their trespasses against them, and entrusting the message of reconciliation to us. So we are ambassadors for Christ, since God is making his appeal through us; we entreat you on behalf of Christ, be reconciled to God. For our sake he made him to be sin who knew no sin, so that in him we might become the righteousness of God. (2 Corinthians 5:13–21)

I have said these things to you while I am still with you. But the Advocate, the Holy Spirit, whom the Father will send in my name, will teach you everything, and remind you of all that I have said to you. Peace I leave with you; my peace I give to you. I do not give to you as the world gives. Do not let your hearts be troubled, and do not let them be afraid. You heard me say to you, "I am going away, and I am coming to you." (John 14:25–28)

Beloved, I am writing you no new commandment, but an old commandment that you have had from the beginning; the old commandment is the word that you have heard. Yet I am writing you a new commandment that is true in him and in you, because the darkness is passing away and the true light is already shining. Whoever says, "I am in the light," while hating a brother or sister, is still in the darkness. Whoever loves a brother or sister lives in the light, and in such a person there is no cause for stumbling. (1 John 2:7–10)

GUIDED MEDITATION

Imagine you are sitting in a comfortable lawn chair facing a meadow. Behind you stands Jesus, his two hands resting on your shoulders. You feel the loving warmth of his love flow from his hands into your shoulders, your chest, all of you, body and soul. Rest a few moments in this love that flows through you. Others join Jesus. These are the people who have loved you well with whom you are now at peace. They lift up their hands toward you in blessing. Among them perhaps are close relatives, grandparents, and others who loved you well. The love of God pours through them also. You feel the comfort of the moment, the strength of the moment, the "at homeness" of the moment.

Now, let there pass in front of you someone you care about, but with whom you are conflicted. Look at their face, their eyes, and their body stance. What do you feel is going on in them? Try for a moment to sense what their life is like right now. Speak to the person directly, reflecting back, acknowledging what must be going on inside of them. Affirm the good you see in that person. How do they react to your words? What do they say in return?

Come up with a word picture to show how their behavior has affected you. Start off with the words, "I feel as if…"

Using a word picture, briefly tell them how you would like to see their behavior change and how you might change your own behavior. Recall a time when your relationship was closer and more peaceful, undisturbed by the current conflict. Tell them you would like to return to that kind of relationship. Close by assuring them of your love and asking forgiveness, if you feel forgiveness is needed.

Try this every time you have a conflict with another, before talking with them about it. I think you will find your words to be healing words when you finally talk to them in real life.

QUESTIONS FOR JOURNALING

1. Write about a time you had a conflict with someone and you worked through the conflict to peace. What did this feel like?
2. Write about a time your temper got out of control and caused pain. What might you do differently now?
3. Write the story of when someone you care about confronted you lovingly about a conflict and you left feeling loved, affirmed, and built up.

~chapter nine~

LOVING
Our Neighbor Means
Offering Forgiveness

The sacrifice acceptable to God is a broken spirit;
a broken and contrite heart, O God, you will not
despise. (Psalm 51:17)

Archbishop Desmond Tutu wrote a memoir of the Truth and Reconciliation Commission delving into the atrocities committed in South Africa under Apartheid. The book's compelling title is *No Future without Forgiveness*. That same phrase can be applied to all of us. None of us has a future without forgiveness.

One definition of forgiveness is refusing to allow negativity into our hearts and relationships because of something someone has done to us. As David Hegg has put it, "To remain unforgiving, which we think of as a right we should enjoy, is actually to inflict deepening pain and erosion of spirit on ourselves. To forgive is better by far."[39]

Forgiving others is a healing event for us. Leo Buscaglia tells the story of a woman who was raped and beaten around the head. She suffered blindness due to her injuries. On a TV interview program, the host asked her if she felt bitterness toward the perpe-trator, for what she suffered. She replied, "Oh, no! That man took one night of my life. I refuse to give him one additional second!"[40]

To have peace in our souls we need to forgive. I heard a wonderful story on one of my retreats of how forgiveness brought peace of soul and reconciliation between two estranged sisters.

Eva lay terrified in her bed in cardiac ICU after a massive heart attack. She was totally alone. It was not something she had ever anticipated, yet here she was. Her husband of forty years had died three years before. Their one child, Billy, had died in a car acci-dent twenty years earlier. At the age of seventy, she was retired from her profession as an attorney and had no close friends. She hated the isolation of living alone; it was almost too much for her to endure. Yet she had no options.

Eva's one sibling, her younger sister Mary, lived in another part of the city, but they barely spoke. The two sisters had been close until Mary entered high school. Eva was the studious one, making straight As. Mary paid little attention to her schoolwork, but paid lots of attention to boys, her social life, and the most stylish clothes. Mary had people skills, but not academic skills. In addition, their parents seemed to favor Mary. Despite her achieve-ments, Eva felt left out, slighted. She resented all the attention Mary received.

Finally the two sisters experienced a stormy estrangement when they were in their late forties. When their widowed mother became too feeble to live alone, Eva took charge. She arranged for their mother to get the finest care at an expensive assisted living facility, which Eva would pay for. Then Mary rushed in and offered to care for their mother in her own modest home, an offer their mother immediately accepted.

Eva boiled over with rage. She cornered her sister and stormed at her, "You know she'll get the best care in assisted living. You're not a responsible person, you've never been responsible. You are doing this just to collect mother's life insurance and her savings. As far as I am concerned, I no longer have a sister."

Mary responded with equally hard words. During the two subsequent years their mother lived, Eva dutifully dropped by to visit her mother at Mary's every two weeks, but her manner was aloof and barely civil.

After their mother's death, Eva stopped all contact with Mary. Yet each Christmas and on each of her birthdays Eva would get a card from Mary saying, "I love you and I'm praying for you." Mary was doing her best to keep up some contact with Eva.

Her second morning in ICU, Eva woke up and found a woman standing beside her with tears in her eyes. The face was familiar, but Eva just couldn't make it out. Then the woman's hand brushed her forehead and she whispered softly, "Eva, I love you. I love you more than you can know." It was Mary. Eva was not alone. The troubles and resentments of decades washed away. They were simply two sisters who loved each other.

Mary remained by Eva's side every day; it was as though there had never been a breach in their relationship. When she was discharged from the hospital, Mary took Eva into her own home to recuperate. Mary's faith had deepened over the many years and her forgiveness for her sister had deepened, too. That forgiveness had just needed the right time to manifest itself.

When we don't forgive others, that failure to forgive can turn into resentment, and few things wound like resentment. When we hold on to resentment, we are the ones who hurt. Max Lucado calls resentment the "cocaine of emotions." It revs people up. It energizes them. It addicts them. We can become addicted to our own resentments. Have you ever seen someone seem to come alive and take pleasure in telling how others have done them wrong? Persistent resentment can become a false but all-consuming pleasure. People can come to enjoy their resentment.

Resentment is about power and control. It is a drug that inebriates; few things deliver the mighty rush of power that hurting others can deliver. And yet, resentment also rips us apart. It wrecks our relationships. When we resent, we no longer have time to breathe in the freshness of each moment. We cease to see the beauty in the world. Hatred leaves little room for love of any sort. When we resent, we push away those who love us, even those who have never hurt us and never will. At times we can even push away God with our resentment.

One reason people hesitate to forgive is that they think forgiveness and reconciliation are the same thing. Actually, they are quite different. Forgiveness involves the process of letting go of the negative emotions that can come with feeling hurt. Forgiveness happens in our relationship with God, without contact with the offender. Jesus captured this beautifully when he said, "Whenever you stand praying, forgive, if you have anything against anyone; so that your Father in heaven may forgive you your trespasses" (Mark 11:25).

The first step in breaking this pattern and forgiving others is to realize how much God has forgiven us personally. God is a lavish forgiver. Coming to him often to be forgiven teaches us about how we should forgive others. That great evangelical preacher of the nineteenth century, Henry Ward Beecher, said, "God forgives like a parent who kisses the offense into everlasting forgetfulness."[41]

God's forgiveness does for the human heart what sunshine does for a plant, it warms it and causes it to grow. Our hearts become compassionate and ready to forgive. Sadly, the idea of going to God to be forgiven holds little popularity today, even in many churches. In today's society, it is much easier to blame others for our failings, to count all the ways we have been wronged and use those wrongs as excuses for our current failings. In our own minds, if we are no longer responsible for our actions and our feelings, we need never seek forgiveness. Instead we say, "My past made me do this; the unfairness of the world has left me unable to take control of my life."

A young man addicted to alcohol, instead of taking responsibility for his actions by seeking treatment and the lavish forgiveness of God might instead complain, "I can't help myself. My father didn't pay enough attention to me when I was little. He rarely came to my Little League games." It is so easy for adult children to blame sins and failings on their parents or on other factors rather than to seek forgiveness and admit their own failings. His father probably should have gone to more of his baseball games and shown him more attention, but at some point we have to take responsibility for our own actions. I once heard a saying, "No matter how many times you fail, you don't become a failure till you blame someone else."

Forgiveness always involves at least some forgetting. We don't deny the hurt done to us, repress it, or minimize it. Instead, with God's help and the help of others, we grieve, let go, and move on. We no longer allow the hurt done to us, or the person who did the hurting, to control us.

Forgiveness is usually not instantaneous. It is a process. It takes time. Just wanting to start down the journey toward forgiveness is enough in God's eyes. God's forgiveness toward us is like a canceled banknote, burned and written off the books. That's what God's forgiveness is like. He forgets the wrong for all eternity.

Once I heard a story of a Filipino priest, a devout man who prayed frequently and was a healing force within his congregation. It seems that in seminary he committed a serious sin that, in his mind, was so bad that he had never told anyone about it outside the confessional.

In his parish there was a woman reputed to have visions of Jesus in her dreams. As was prudent, the priest was skeptical about her visionary claims. One day after weekday morning Mass, wanting to test the genuineness of her visions, he asked her if Jesus had appeared to her in her dreams the night before. When she said he had, the priest asked her, "The next time Jesus appears to you at night, ask him to tell you what the sin was I committed in seminary."

He didn't see the woman for several days. When he finally saw her, he asked, "Has Jesus appeared to you again?"

She answered, "Yes."

"Did you ask him what sin I committed in seminary?" he continued.

"Yes."

"Well, what did he say?"

The woman answered, "He said, 'I forget.'"

Take time each day to tell God about the shadows of your soul. If you are Catholic or Orthodox, you can complete and seal that forgiveness by frequenting the sacrament of reconciliation. As we experience God's forgiveness, we will begin to forgive others in our life as freely as God forgives us.

In forgiving others it is important to acknowledge the wrongs that have been done to us or those we care about. This acknowledgment can mean feeling and working through feelings of revenge, injury, and hurt. As Lewis Smedes said, "Forgiveness is a journey, the deeper the wound, the longer the journey."[42]

The next step in forgiveness is learning to bless the one you might now resent. Jesus says: "Love your enemies and pray for those who persecute you, so that you may be children of your Father in heaven" (Matthew 5:44–45). Begin to pray for that person. Hard as it may be, begin to see that person as a child of God, just as you are. Imagine what that person's world is like. Think of the pain that person endured that led them to hurt instead of help. Begin the process of seeing the person as a struggling child of God, like you. Empathize with them. Walk a mile in their shoes. What is their day like? What happened in their past? Seven hundred years ago, Thomas à Kempis wrote in *The Imitation of Christ,* "Know all and you will pardon all."[43]

Knowledge has personally helped me in forgiving. Growing up I was a puzzle to those around me because of my cerebral disability. Except for a moderate speech impairment, I came across as highly intelligent. When it came to ideas, concepts, and words, some said I was years ahead of my age. Yet sequential tasks and visual-spatial ability were significantly impaired. When I got a thorough diagnosis at one of the premier brain injury centers in the country, one of the measures of my difficulty was the Wechsler personally administered intelligence test. There was a forty-five–point gap between my verbal IQ, which was near genius, and my performance IQ, which was on the borderline of disabled. I seemed bright, yet tasks like dressing and keeping anything neat and in order was a near impossibility. Everything I touched looked messy and thoughtless.

When I was growing up, long before my diagnosis, Mother could not control her rage or harsh words. She interpreted my problems as laziness and would shame me. Thousands of times, it seems, she told me that if I didn't change soon, I would grow up to be a failure. Soon, even when Mother was calm, I began repeating those same things to myself. I felt dirty, inadequate, and ashamed. I thought if I only had the willpower, I could surmount my problems and be like others. If I could say worse things to myself than my mother and teachers, their words would not hurt as much. I use to wear a rubber band on my wrist that I would pop often and say to myself, "Eddie, you are no good at all."

Yet despite the harsh words I often heard I never ceased believing my parents loved me. They both showered me with hugs and kisses. At times, they could be quite tender, telling me how much they loved me. They never laid a hand on me. I understood, even when I was a child, that much of my mother's rage came from her mother's untimely death and being abandoned in an orphanage by her father. Daddy's paranoia and delusions came from a mental illness he could not help.

My successes in winning state-wide and local essay contests and oratorical contests during high school led to my parents becoming genuinely proud of me. The year I studied French they took me on an educational trip to Quebec City and Montreal. Another year they took me to Williamsburg. I was as perplexed as they were as to the cause of my disability. When I began to fail at some things in my early adulthood they always welcomed me back home.

Yet, through the years, my inner dialogue of shame that had come from their rage did not cease. I still felt lazy, and at times a failure, even after earning a masters' degree and a doctorate, writing books, and speaking to thousands of people on spirituality. I needed to go further with my forgiveness of them.

The first step was my acknowledging that the hurt and shame I felt were not real. They were not the reality of who I was. Then I needed to tell others about my difficulties with my parents growing up. Letting go of the secrets was a key part of this. I told my parents about my disability when it was first diagnosed, but it was difficult for them to grasp. In my book *Visions* that came out in 2000, after my father's death, I told the story of how difficult life was for me as a child with a hard to understand disability.

I gave my mother a copy. Soon after she began reading it, she called to tell me, with tears sounding through her voice, "I understand now. I understand what life was like for you growing up. It must have been so hard for you. And yes, though you didn't mention it in the book, I would get so angry at you for something you could not help."

After she finished, I told her I would be at her house soon. After I entered the door, she surrounded me with a firm, warm embrace. We held each other, both sobbing.

"It must have been so hard for you."

"It was, Mother, it was," I replied. "But I have a spiritual announcement to make: I have the best mother in the world."

"And I have the best son," she added.

We lingered in the embrace a while, our hearts resting in a profound love and reconciliation.

Reconciliation can happen when the one who caused the hurt acknowledges their role, offers to change, and seeks a restored relationship. Going to the offender when the time is right, with a heart that has already forgiven, speeds that process. Part of reconciliation means risk, the risk of being hurt again. It means having a heart to restore the relationship.

Reconciliation after the little daily ways we hurt each other should be an everyday event. Reconciliation after serious abuse is more problematic. It involves time, healing, and often professional help. In some instances where serious harm has been done, forgiveness is possible, but not reconciliation, at least this side of glory.

As G.K. Chesterton put it, "To love means loving the unlovable. To forgive means pardoning the unpardonable. Faith means believing the unbelievable. Hope means hoping when everything seems hopeless."[44]

When we forgive someone, healing bursts forth within us. Max Lucado states it beautifully:

> God wants you to fly. He wants you to fly free of yesterday's guilt. He wants you to fly free of today's fears. He wants you to fly free of tomorrow's grave. Sin, fear, and death. These are the mountains he has moved. These are the prayers he will answer. That is the fruit he will grant. This is what he longs to do: he longs to set you free so you can fly...home.[45]

We need to forgive to have peace in our souls and to let the past be truly past.

TIME FOR HEALING PRAYER
A Prayer

Dear Lord, your forgiveness is the medicine that heals, the salve that calms, the touch that mends. Help me candidly acknowledge my sinfulness, ways that I have hurt you or others, and ways that I have broken your commands. Help me to pour out to you any bitterness that I may harbor in my soul. I call upon your compassionate heart to help me forgive others as lavishly as you have forgiven me. Give me the wisdom of how to reconcile with others, when reconciliation is possible. Amen.

SCRIPTURE TO PONDER

Read this over, out loud if possible, savor the words, let them sink and plant themselves in the innermost part of your heart.

Then Peter came and said to him, "Lord, if another member of the church sins against me, how often should I forgive? As many as seven times?" Jesus said to him, "Not seven times, but, I tell you, seventy-seven times.

"For this reason the kingdom of heaven may be compared to a king who wished to settle accounts with his slaves. When he began the reckoning, one who owed him ten thousand talent was brought to him; and, as he could not pay, his lord ordered him to be sold, together with his wife and children and all his possessions, and payment to be made. So the slave fell on his knees before him, saying, 'Have patience with me, and I will pay you everything.'

"And out of pity for him, the lord of that slave released him and forgave him the debt. But that same slave, as he went out, came upon one of his fellow-slaves who owed him a hundred denarii; and seizing him by the throat, he said, 'Pay what you owe' Then his fellow-slave fell down and pleaded with him, 'Have patience with me, and I will pay you.' But he refused; then he went and threw him into prison until he should pay the debt. When his fellow-slaves saw what had happened, they were greatly distressed, and they went and reported to their lord all that had taken place. Then his lord summoned him and said to him, 'You wicked slave! I forgave you all that debt because you pleaded with me. Should you not have had mercy on your fellow-slave, as I had mercy on you?' And in anger his lord handed him over to be tortured until he should pay his entire debt. So my heavenly Father will also do to every one of you, if you do not forgive your brother or sister from your heart." (Matthew 18:21–35)

Guided Meditation

Part One: Seat yourself in a comfortable chair and take time to grow still. Perhaps repeat the Jesus Prayer. The love of God fills the room. You feel someone grasp your shoulders from behind. It is Jesus. Peace, calm, and assurance flow from his hands into you. You feel safe, so very safe. Take time to remember the last time you experienced the release of forgiveness. Perhaps it was the relief and joy of experiencing the sacrament of reconciliation. Maybe it was a time someone in your life reached far inside their hearts and forgave you. Experience again the peace of that moment.

Now Jesus moves from behind your chair and sits in a chair facing you. He takes your two hands in his. You know he wants you to search your heart for ways that you have hurt yourself, God, or others; for times that you have broken God's commandments. Tell him about your sins and experience his tender compassion and forgiveness. If you are Catholic or Orthodox, complete this act of contrition by celebrating the sacrament of reconciliation.

Part Two: You are seated in a chair; behind you is Jesus, holding your shoulders. It is so very safe to be there with Jesus. In front of you is an empty seat.

Now picture someone you have been close to you, but who has hurt you deeply, step in and sit in that seat facing you. What feelings do you have? Remember Jesus is there, protecting and comforting you. His strong hands are on your shoulders, keeping you calm.

Forgiveness is a process, not an instant event. Are you ready to begin the process of forgiveness with the person in front of you? It's OK if you are not ready. Jesus can help you begin that process later in your life when you are ready.

If you think you are ready to begin, look into the person's eyes, and survey their face. What pain and difficulty in life do you think shaped them? Try to see the world from that person's perspective. You hear the person ask you, "What could I have done to love you better?"

Tell that person what they could have done to love you better. Only if you feel ready, tell them you are ready to begin the process of forgiving him or her. Only if you feel safe doing so, walk up to the person and clasp that person's hands in affection. Jesus comes and joins the two of you, placing a hand on your shoulder while placing a hand on the other person's shoulder.

Questions for Journaling

1. Can you think of a time you felt abundantly loved by God? If so, write about it.
2. Write about a time another person forgave you from the heart. What did that feel like?
3. Is there someone in your life whom you need to forgive? Write about it.

~chapter ten~

LOVING
Our Neighbor
through Kindness

Few things carry the ability to change our world as simply being kind. Kindness shows love in action. Theologian Albert Outler once said, "The world hears the Gospel when it sees it."[46]

Jesus gave concrete examples of the type of kindness he calls all his children to offer. It was giving a cup of cold water, offering aid to someone who was beaten and left to suffer in a ditch, visiting prisoners, feeding the hungry, clothing those without clothes, and visiting the ill and the prisoner. His life and teachings show a great generosity of spirit and kindness.

In chapter seven of Luke's Gospel we hear that a Pharisee invited Jesus to a supper and a known prostitute crashed the gathering. With great tenderness, she washed Jesus's feet with her tears and dried them with her hair, kissed his feet, and poured sweet smelling oil over them. The Pharisee protested fiercely. "If this man were a prophet, he would know what kind of woman she is" (see Luke 7:39).

Jesus answered, "Two men owed money to a certain money-lender. One owed him a great deal; the other, much less. He canceled the debts of both. Which of them will love him more?" (see Luke 7:43).

Jesus saw past her sin to her wounded heart. He knew that kindness could heal what blame could not.

We are able to show kindness to others because God is so remarkably kind to us. His love is full of kindness. Kindness is part and parcel of the love of God for man. "For the mountains may depart, and the hills be removed; but my kindness shall not depart from you...says the Lord, who has compassion on you." (Isaiah 54:10).

Since God's love flows over with kindness, kindness flows unstoppably from the center of his heart. It is in his nature to be kind. And when we open up our hearts to that kindness, it trains our hearts to act in kind ways, letting our hearts overflow to others with the same kindness God shows us.

Acts of kindness mean far more in God's eyes than a large retirement account, professional success, or our popularity. Jesus demonstrated his kindness by healing the sick and showing compassion to the sinner. In a mighty act of kindness, while suffering on the cross, he shows generosity to the thief suffering beside him.

Kindness is a cornerstone of virtually every religion. There are more than two hundred references to kindness, helping, and serving others in the Bible. I remember hearing a parable about a modern-day pastor famous for his books and polished ability to preach. The pastor dreamed one night he went to heaven and met an angel who was the gatekeeper. "I have touched many thousands with my books and preaching," he told the angel.

The angel looked and couldn't find his name in the book of life and found no mention of the pastor for preaching and writing.

After looking harder, he found a notation that the pastor had stayed up all night caring for a dying woman. His simple act of kindness meant far more in heaven than all his teaching and writing.

And our acts of kindness don't need to be spectacular to make a real difference. Mother Teresa offers some insights into kindness. "Do not imagine," says Mother Teresa, "that love to be true must be extraordinary.... See how a lamp burns by the continual consumption of the little drops of oil. If there are no more of these drops in the lamp, there will be no light, and the Bridegroom has a right to say: 'I do not know you.'

"My children, what are these drops of oil in our lamps? They are the little things of everyday life: fidelity, punctuality, little words of kindness, just a little thought for others, those little acts of silence, of look and thought, of word and deed. These are the very drops of love that make our religious life burn with so much light. Do not search for Jesus in far off lands," she concludes, "He is not there. He is in you. Just keep the lamps burning and you will always see Him."[47]

One of the finest acts of kindness that can transform other people is affirmation. Affirmation has a way of rearranging us and making us over inside. This type of kindness is the medicine that can cure our ills and transform our lives. Mark Twain once said, "I can live two months on one compliment."[48]

Kindness can reach in and change souls. A beautiful illustration of this comes from Victor Hugo's novel *Les Miserables* (perhaps most familiar to people through the movie or musical versions).

Jean Valjean, an orphan, works hard as a teen to support his widowed sister and her seven children. Even his best effort is not enough to put food on the table of the starving family. In desperation he steals a loaf of bread only to be caught and hauled off to prison. There, under brutal conditions, his young mind becomes filled with hatred, bitterness, and thoughts of revenge. After spending half his life in prison Jean is released, but due to his criminal past, he is shunned everywhere he goes. This hardens his heart even further.

He stumbles on the house of a compassionate bishop who gives him a meal and lets him spend the night. That night he gathers up the bishop's fine silver and leaves. Apprehended by police they take him back to the bishop's house. The bishop warmly greets him then tells the police that he gave the silver to Jean freely. Jean can't understand why he would be so kind to a thief like himself. The bishop lets him know why with these words, "Jean Valjean, my brother, you no longer belong to the evil, but to good. I have bought your soul for you. I withdrew it from black thoughts and the spirit of hate, and gave it to God." Jean leaves the bishop's house a changed man, transfigured by kindness.[49]

The greatest key to enjoying friendship and love from others is to, warmly and honestly, tell them about the beauty we see in them. This open expression of genuine emotion can unlock many new doors and become a transfiguring moment for all. I know because kindness and affirmation changed my life.

As I mentioned earlier in the book, I grew up with a cognitive disability. Tasks that involved sequencing or visual-spatial skills were difficult and confusing. My handwriting was almost illegible, I had a hard time holding numbers in memory, and did poorly at math and science. I needed help dressing and with daily tasks. My parents loved me, but they did not know of my yet undiagnosed disability, nor seek the medical help needed to find it. Instead they blamed me, each in their unique way, raging at me, calling me lazy and a failure. My mother once said to me, "I had such hopes for you when you were a baby. It's hard to have a child like you grow to disappoint me." In addition, I lived in terror because of Daddy's mental illness and paranoia.

School offered no solace. Some of my junior high teachers berated me for my learning disabilities. One junior high teacher told me, "Eddie, you are no good at all." I felt like my life was over before it had really begun.

Despite all this, my verbal skills were excellent. I read two or three years beyond my grade level. I expressed myself beautifully orally.

Only acts of kindness and affirmation saved me. My first year in high school, my English teacher, Helen Hayes, took the time to decipher my handwriting. The essay I wrote on Voltaire came back to me with an A+ on it. She took me aside and told me, "You have great skill as a writer. I want to nourish that. Furthermore it is rare that a fifteen-year-old would be reading Voltaire."

Unknown to me she passed on the essay to Margaret Cox, the dean and guidance counselor, who was starting up a specialized class with Mrs. Hayes for creative students. Designed for students who showed the gift of creativity in their work, the class would be informal and focused on creative writing.

Immediately Miss Cox focused on me, loving my poems and stories despite the messy handwriting. She told me when I grew up I would write many books. Before I completed high school Miss Cox wanted me to be a published writer, and I was, in a statewide teachers' magazine.

I blossomed because of the constant affirmation of these two teachers. Soon a social studies teacher, Helen Shepherd, a close friend of both Mrs. Hayes and Miss Cox joined in. Despite my disability and a bit of a speech impediment, she coached me till I went on to win local then statewide oratorical contests. All three teachers pushed me to do more than get by. They wanted me to excel.

They all sensed my emotions were unsteady, though I could not bring myself to tell them why. It was still in the days when teachers could show affection to students. Margaret Cox and Helen Shepherd greeted me often with warm hugs and a kiss on the cheek, tactile affection I desperately needed at that point in my life. Miss Cox had me often in her counseling office just to chat about the struggles of being a student. Not knowing my home life, she sensed something was askew. She called my parents into her office.

"I called them in," she told me, "to tell them that in you they had a treasure to be cherished and that both my teachers and my parents needed to work together to nurture the gifts I had." She told my parents that she was going to act as my second mother to be sure I was affirmed and nurtured.

My parents made a hundred and eighty degree turn in how they saw and treated me. More and more, like my teachers, they affirmed me, doing things to help me such as hiring a speech therapist to help me transcend my speech impediment so that I could go on to win oratorical contests. Moreover, for the first time, my parents seemed genuinely proud of me.

Children will respond to kindness just as ducks take to water. If immersed in an atmosphere of kindness, children will drink it up and simply find the experience irresistible.

The founder and president of The Acts of Kindness Association said, "Kindness changes hearts, melts away differences, solves problems, and builds bridges instead of barriers."[50]

It changes us not only when others are kind to us, but also when we are kind to others.

I remember the story of a priest I met while conducting a parish retreat in the Midwest. Fr. Ralph, one of the kindest and most loving people I have ever met, grew up in a dysfunctional home. His father was an alcoholic retired sergeant, and what Fr. Ralph describes as a "rage-aholic" with a wild temper. He would go into rants at Ralph for perceived wrongdoing such as a shirt not completely tucked in. Often fists and flailing hands that hurt accompanied his rage. Ralph's mother loved him tenderly, but never intervened, fearing her own safety.

Bright, Ralph escaped by entering into a world of books and by overachieving at school. He found a degree of solace during Mass at his parish, where he was an altar server, but other than good grades, little went well for Ralph. Because of the constant abuse at home, he shut his emotions down.

In his teen years, he desperately wanted friends just as most young people do. However, the thought of sharing his emotions with others, the key to good friendship, terrified him. He was afraid of doing or saying anything among others for fear of causing anger and rage and being emotionally slapped down, the way his father physically slapped him down. He retreated to a lonely place far down inside himself and constructed a wall to keep others away. When he did talk to peers it was only about books and articles. His schoolmates perceived him as haughty, cold, and aloof and usually rebuffed his attempts at conversation.

Ralph grew desperate for companionship but had no idea how to go about it.

Because of his positive experience as an altar server and because of the consolation he received at Mass, he decided to study to become a priest and entered minor seminary. He hoped to make friends among his new classmates since they all shared a common desire to serve the Church. But no matter how much he wanted friends, just willing it could not cut through his ingrained aloofness. He saw his confreres enjoying a game of baseball together and happily going into town for movies together. He desperately wished he could interact with them. Unlike his classmates in high school, his fellow seminarians invited him to come along with them to the movies and other recreational events. Feeling a knot of fear in his throat every time he was asked, he always responded with "No, I have too much schoolwork."

One night, hiding in his room, hearing the sounds of laughter and joy coming from the hall and open doors of other seminarians, his isolation bore down on him like a huge boulder. He could no longer hold off his emotions and collapsed, sobbing uncontrollably in his padded chair. Even a pillow held to his face could not control the noise of his keening.

Soon he heard a knock at his bedroom door. He didn't open up. Then two voices grew insistent outside his door, one from Dave and the other from John, two of the friendliest of his classmates.

"Ralph, let us in!" Dave shouted.

"We are not going away, even if we have to stand here knocking all night," vowed John.

Reluctantly Ralph opened he door and then stepped back. To Ralph's surprise, the two young men said nothing at first. Instead, they enveloped him in an embrace. As they did so his sobs became even stronger. Finally Dave asked, tenderly but firmly, "What's wrong?"

Ralph could no longer hold back, "I am so alone. I have no one. No one cares."

"We do," said Dave and John in unison. Somehow their words got through to him and he relaxed further in their arms.

They held him fifteen minutes while his sobs subsided. John led them in one Our Father; then they all sat down.

"From now on when we go out for pizza or a movie, you come with us, we won't take no as your answer," they told him.

Ralph's life was changed because two young seminarians showed that they cared. The other seminarians joined in too; making sure he joined with them in recreation and outings. A slow metamorphosis came over Ralph and for the first time in his life he became part of a network of people who cared.

Dave and John encouraged Ralph to share his feelings of isolation with his spiritual director. He did, and his spiritual director suggested he also start seeing a counselor to help him work through his past.

Ralph blossomed. He developed what he called a "spirituality of kindness" for himself. Daily in his morning meditation, he envisioned ways he could show kindness and love to everyone he met. He shared the kindness that had changed his life with countless others, changing the course of their lives, too.

If you want to become kind, pray. In prayer we can allow God to pour his kindness into our hearts. His kindness readies us to show kindness to others. Soaking in God's kindness changes us on an inner level so that kindness becomes part of our nature. It's easier, then, to do little loving things for others.

Fr. Ralph's idea of a "spirituality of kindness," is rooted deep in Scripture and tradition. Each prayer time we have we can review the day, visualizing the people we might meet and practicing being kind to them in our meditations. When we do this we let kindness seep into the subterranean depths of our souls, opening us wide to that One Love that undergirds all that is.

TIME FOR HEALING PRAYER
A Prayer

Dear Lord, you have shown your immense kindness to us in your consolation and in your mercy. In the sacraments your kindness touches us, embraces us in tangible ways, and calls to us to let our words and actions toward others become sacraments of your presence. Keep us always close to your heart and through showing kindness bring others into your heart. Amen.

SCRIPTURE TO PONDER

As God's chosen ones, holy and beloved, clothe your-selves with compassion, kindness, humility, meekness, and patience. Bear with one another and, if anyone has a complaint against another, forgive each other; just as the Lord has forgiven you, so you also must forgive. (Colossians 3:12–13)

Remind them to be subject to rulers and authorities, to be obedient, to be ready for every good work, to speak evil of no one, to avoid quarrelling, to be gentle, and to show every courtesy to everyone. For we ourselves were once foolish, disobedient, led astray, slaves to various passions and pleasures, passing our days in malice and envy, despi-cable, hating one another. But when the goodness and loving-kindness of God our Savior appeared, he saved us, not because of any works of righteousness that we had done, but according to his mercy, through the water of rebirth and renewal by the Holy Spirit. This Spirit he poured out on us richly through Jesus Christ our Savior, so that, having been justified by his grace, we might become heirs according to the hope of eternal life. (Titus 3:1–7)

GUIDED MEDITATION
Part One: Affirming Oneself

How many times have you heard the phrase, "To love others you must learn to love yourself?" Since kindness is a part of love, being kind to others means, in part, being kind to ourselves. Most of us have heard this so many times that it has become a cliché. However, many of us have found that loving ourselves is not an easy matter!

A key part of loving ourselves and being kind to ourselves is seeing our inner goodness, learning to affirm ourselves. Many times we are overcome with self-criticism, self-doubt, and fear. At times these emotions paralyze us. Learning to affirm ourselves is a key to establishing strong loving relationships with others.

Our self-image, that is, how we see ourselves and how we feel about ourselves, is often complex and multifaceted. Affirmations and creative visualization are wonderful ways of creating a more positive and loving self-image.

The following prayer experience is one to help you grow in the art of loving yourself. It is often easy to appreciate the good qualities in others and to see their faults and shortcomings in perspective. We are usually harder on ourselves. Loving yourself can work wonders in your life.

Take time to relax and be still. Then review your day so far. Or if it's morning, review yesterday. Think about how you felt at different times during the day. Just notice what ideas and images you held about yourself at different times. See if you notice overly critical, harsh judgments about yourself. Notice their power to ensnare you and to harm you.

Picture a helium balloon whose gondola is a big trash can. In your imagination take these harsh judgments of yourself—as though you were pulling them from your stomach or chest area—and deposit them into the trash can, one by one.

Now take a knife and cut the ropes that are holding down the trash can and the balloon and see those harsh self-judgments float away. Feel yourself feeling light and joyous as they float away.

Imagine that you are in an everyday situation. Someone comes to you with a look of love and affirmation to tell you something very good about yourself. More people join in. They tell you how much they like you and what a good person you are. Soak in what they say. More and more people come and look on you with love and respect in their eyes. What sort of good things do they say about you?

Rest now. Rest a moment in the sense of self-worth that you feel, realizing deeply that God made you and that he made you good.

Part Two: Affirming Others

One of the finest acts of kindness that can transform others is affirmation. The greatest key to enjoying friendship and love from others is to, warmly and honestly, tell them about the beauty we see in them. This open expression of genuine emotion can unlock many new doors and become a transfiguring experience for all.

In the following passage, Paul encourages the people in the Church at Philippi, and he lets them know that he also remembers and affirms them in his prayer. For your Scripture journey, do what Paul did.

> I thank my God every time I remember you, constantly praying with joy in every one of my prayers for all of you, because of your sharing in the gospel from the first day until now. I am confident of this, that the one who began a good work among you will bring it to completion by the day of Jesus Christ.
>
> It is right for me to think this way about all of you, because you hold me in your heart, for all of you share in God's grace with me, both in my imprisonment and in the defense and confirmation of the gospel. For God is my witness, how I long for all of you with the compassion of Christ Jesus. (Philippians 1:3–8)

Picture yourself affirming other people in your prayer in the same manner as Paul. Think about how God's grace has touched them. Experience the goodness that God has poured into them. Let yourself yearn deeply for the completion of their journey in God's grace.

Relax. Now allow different people in your life to emerge into your imagination, one at a time. Look into their eyes. Be aware of the goodness you see in them and tell them. What change does your telling them make in the look on their faces? Be aware of how it affects how they relate to you. Notice the effect on your own heart as a result of this open, beautiful honesty. Be still and rest in this good feeling.

QUESTIONS FOR JOURNALING

1. What are some of the times others have shown you kindness and it changed your life?
2. Think of some of the times you have experienced God's kindness and write about them.
3. What can you do to share kindness with others?

~notes~

1. "Two Kinds of Healing," *Sarasota Herald-Tribune* (Florida) March 14, 1996, Sarasota Venice Manatee Edition.

2. "Divorce Rate and Divorce Statistics in the USA," http://www.divorcestatistics.info/divorce-statistics-and-divorce-rate-in-the-usa.html.

3. Augustine of Hippo, *On the Trinity*, chapter 9, paragraph 12.

4. Quoted in Diana Hagee, *The Romance of Redemption* (Nashville: Thomas Nelson, 2005), p. 161.

5. "Requiem for a Nun," Wikipedia, http://en.wikipedia.org/wiki/Requiem_for_a_Nun.

6. Martin Luther King, Jr., "Sermon delivered at Dexter Ave. Baptist Church, Montgomery, AL, November 17, 1957," http://www.ipoet.com/ARCHIVE/BEYOND/King-Jr/Loving-Your-Enemies.html.

7. "Writing Our Troubles Away," *Austin American-Statesman* (Texas), March 1, 1998.

8. Aelred of Rievaulx, *A Friend in God*, trans. Tom Noe, (Amazon Digital Services, Kindle, 2013), loc 404.

9. Keith J. Egan and Lawrence S. Cunningham, *Christian Spirituality* (Mahwah, N.J.: Paulist, 1996), n.p.

10. Augustine, *Confessions*, trans. Albert C. Outler (Mineola, N.Y.: Dover, 2002), p. 163.

11. Thomas Celano, *The Life of St. Francis* (Paterson, N.J.: St. Anthony Guild, 1962), pp. 43–44.

12. Brother Ugolino, *The Little Flowers of St. Francis of Assisi*, XV.

13. Quoted in Lawrence Cunningham and Keith Egan, Christian Spirituality: Themes from the Tradition (Mahwah, N.J.: Paulist, 1996), p. 165.

14. Quoted in William Johnston, *Silent Music: The Science of Meditation* (San Francisco: HarperSanFrancisco, 1997), pp. 160–161.

15. Aelred of Rievaulx, quoted at http://www.christianity.org.uk/index.php/a/loneliness.php#whattheysay.

16. Patrick F. Fagan, Ph.D., "Why Religion Matters Even More: The Impact of Religious Practice on Social Stability," *The Heritage Foundation*, http://www.heritage.org/research/reports/2006/12/why-religion-matters-even-more-the-impact-of-religious-practice-on-social-stability.

17. Gregory Wolfe and Suzanne Wolfe, *Circle of Grace* (New York: Ballantine, 2000), p. 43.

18. Dr. William Sears and Martha Sears, *The Successful Child* (New York: Little, Brown, 2002), as quoted in Letitia Suk "Together in Prayer," *Newsday*, section part II, page B01.

19. Kenneth M. Locke, "Family Devotions," *Upper Room*, January/February 1993, p. 61.

20. Dennis Rainey and Barbara Rainey, *Growing Spiritually Strong Families* (Colorado Springs, Colo.: Multnomah, 2002), p. 24.

21. Alphonsus de Liguori, *Selected Writings* (Mahwah, N.J.: Paulist, 1999), p. 284.

22. Rosalind Rinker, *How to Get the Most Out of Prayer Life* (Eugene, Ore.: Harvest House, 1981), p. 31ff.

23. Martin Luther King, Jr., *Measure of a Man* (Philadelphia: Fortress, 2001), p. 42.

24. Marianne E. Roche, *On-the-Job Spirituality: Finding God in Work* (Cincinnati: St. Anthony Messenger Press, 2002), p. 33.

25. Roche, ix.

26. Jeff Zaslow, "Spirituality in the Workplace," *Chicago Sun-Times*, March 31, 2001, Late Sports Edition.

27. Carol Glatz, "Elderly, Sick, Unborn, Poor are 'Masterpieces of God's Creation,'" *Catholic News Service*, July 17, 2013, http://www.catholicnews.com/data/stories/cns/1303071.htm.

28. P.G. Walsh, *The Poems of St. Paulinus of Nola* (Mahwah, N.J.: Paulist, 1974), p. 185.

29. Pope Francis, The Joy of the Gospel (*Evangelii Gaudium*), 198.

30. Raymond Brown, *The Gospel According to John* (New York: Doubleday, 1966–1970), p. 562.

31. "Child Poverty," *National Center for Children in Poverty*, http://www.nccp.org/topics/childpoverty.html.

32. "Pope on Lampedusa: 'The Globalization of Indifference,'" *Vatican Radio*, August 7, 2013, http://en.radiovaticana.va/storico/2013/07/08/pope_on_lampedusa_%E2%80%9Cthe_globalization_ of_indifference%E2%80%9D/en1-708541.

33. Joanna Macy, "Spiritual Practices for Activists," http://www.joannamacy.net/spiritual-practices-for-activists.html.

34. Jonathan Robinson, *Communication Miracles for Couples* (San Francisco: Conari, 2012), p. 21.

35. Cato the Elder, quoted at *Quotations Book*, http://quotationsbook.com/quote/2451/.

36. Carol Tavris, *Anger: The Misunderstood Emotion* (New York: Simon & Schuster, 1989), p. 25.

37. Les Parrott and Leslie Parrott, *The Good Fight* (Grand Rapids: Zondervan, 2011), p. 169.

38. Andrew Santella, "Why So Mad?" *Notre Dame Magazine*, Summer 2007, http://magazine.nd.edu/news/9815-why-so-mad/.

39. Quoted in David Hegg, "Figuring Out Forgiveness—Ethically Speaking," *The Signal* (Santa Clarita, Calif.), September 25, 2010.

40. Leo Buscaglia, *Loving Each Other* (New York: Ballantine, 1986), p. 93.

41. Henry Ward Beecher, quoted at, http://www.famousquotesandauthors.com/authors/henry_ward_beecher_quotes.html.

42. Dr. Marjorie E. Baker, "Forgiveness: What It Is, What It Isn't," *Dayton Daily News* (Ohio), August 5, 2012.

43. Thomas a Kempis, quoted at *World of Quotes*, http://www. worldofquotes.com/quote/13003/index.html.

44. G.K. Chesterton, quoted at *ThinkExist Quotations,* http:// thinkexist.com/quotation/to_love_means_loving_the_unlovable- to_forgive/257857.html.

45. Max Lucado, *And the Angels Were Silent* (Colorado Springs: Multnomah, 2005), p. 72.

46. Quoted by Rev. Timothy J. Smith, "Making it Last," *The Works Dynamic Preaching*, www.sermons.com.

47. Mother Teresa, *The Love of Christ* (New York: Harper & Row, 1982), pp. 73–74.

48. Roy B. Zuck, *The Speaker's Quote Book* (Grand Rapids: Kregel Academic and Professional, 2009), p. 166.

49. William J. Bennett, *The Book of Virtues* (New York: Simon and Schuster, 1993), p. 646.

50. "Editorial: Kindness is the Cure for Nation," *The Times and Democrat* (South Carolina), June 14, 2002. http://thetandd. com/news/opinion/editorial-kindness-is-the-cure-for-nation -association-puts-focus/article_b0191ca3-d2d7-5f35-9a50 -41c1d4c460b8.html.

ABOUT THE AUTHOR

Eddie Ensley is a Catholic permanent deacon from the diocese of Savannah, Georgia. He is part of the clergy staff at St. Anne in Columbus, Georgia. He teaches spirituality at Josephinum Diaconate Institute of the Pontifical College Josephinum. Deacon Ensley is a NCCA licensed clinical pastoral counselor with a master's degree in pastoral studies (Loyola University) and a doctorate in clinical pastoral counseling (Cornerstone University). For more information visit www.parishmission.net.